Praise for *1*

"This wonderful book brings back memories of ~~~~~~~~~~~~~~~ her with respect and dignity. We also developed frie~~~~~~~~~~~~~~ me. Tony and I fought in the ring, but we were both cut ... ~~~~~~~ iave remained close all these years. This book is a tribute to many of us who partic~ ~d in the sport we call boxing."

Carmen Basilio, former Middleweight Champion; former Welterweight Champion

"*Nardo, Memoirs of a Boxing Champion* tells the story of the great Tony DeMarco and not only his life in the ring, but his life in general. Tony was one of my favorite Champs as a fighter and as a man. Tony, I salute you!"

Jake LaMotta "The Raging Bull," former Middleweight Champion

"*Nardo* is a great read and an inspirational story. Many years ago, Tony DeMarco inspired me to become a professional boxer. I tried to emulate this great fighter in every way possible. Sammy Fuller became my trainer, Rip Valenti my manager, and I even trained in the Catskills. I would observe Tony's every move in the ring, the way that he handled himself in public, and the way that he treated other people. Tony was my boxing idol, and to this day has remained a very dear friend. The book gives people the chance to see the man, not just the boxer. At times during my political career, I often thought about Tony's inner strength and courage. This helped me make what I hope were the right decisions when it came to protecting the rights of citizens of the Commonwealth."

Joe DeNucci, former Middleweight Contender and former State Auditor, the Commonwealth of Massachusetts

"The book is a knockout. Both Tony and Rocky had so much in common - especially heart."

Peter Marciano, brother of former undefeated Heavyweight Champ, Rocky Marciano

"Tony DeMarco is a walking reminder of the halcyon days of live gate boxing, where ballyhoo was obligatory and a fighter's heart was compulsory. His 13-year career, which consisted of depths of heartbreak and peaks of euphoria, held him in good stead for what was to come in life."

Dan Hanley, Cyber Boxing Zone

"Back in the early 1950s, a young man from Boston became a rising star in boxing and went on to win the World Welterweight Championship. Tony DeMarco was the "Peoples Champion" because he never forgot his roots. Well-respected in the boxing world, Tony continues to impress fans with his charm, charisma, and his many accomplishments. Boxing gave Tony the opportunity to fight for what is right in this great country we call America. This book tells his story."

Joe Cortez, International Boxing Hall of Fame referee

NARDO

Memoirs of a Boxing Champion

Library of Congress Cataloging-in-Publication Data

DeMarco, Tony, 1932-
  Nardo : memoirs of a boxing champion / by Tony DeMarco with Ellen Zappala.
   p. cm.
  ISBN 1-881901-81-5 (pbk.)
  1. DeMarco, Tony, 1932- 2. Boxers (Sports)--United States--Biography. I. Zappala, Ellen. II. Title.
  GV1132.D375A3 2011
  796.83092--dc23
  [B]
                    2011029201

Acknowledgements

All images courtesy of the Tony DeMarco Collection.

Cover Design: ATS Communications, Merrimac, MA.

Printed in Canada

For information and for orders, write to:

Legas

P. O. Box 149   3 Wood Aster Bay
Mineola, New York   Ottawa, Ontario
11501, USA   K2R 1D3

Legaspublishing.com

NARDO

MEMOIRS OF A BOXING CHAMPION

By

Tony
DeMarco

with Ellen Zappala

The Autobiography of
Undisputed Welterweight Champ, Tony DeMarco
"The Flame & Fury of Fleet Street"

LEGAS

Good Luck
Jack & Lynda

I dedicate this book to my family, friends, and fans.
God's blessings always.

Tony DeMarco

Contents

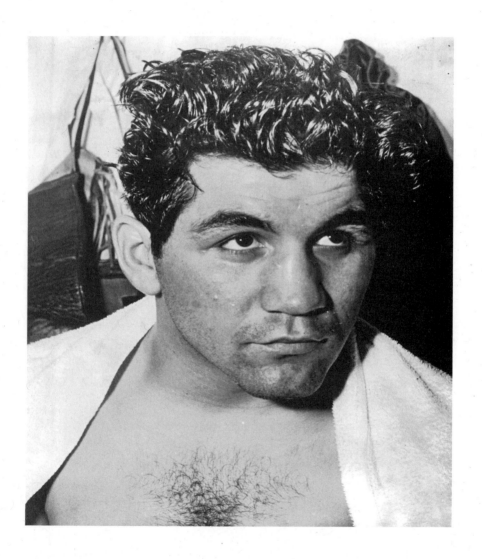

Foreword

My first recollection of Tony DeMarco was in the early 1950s when my uncle Johnny "The Killer" Randazzo, an amateur boxing champion, showed me pictures of not only Tony, but other Italian American boxers who were displayed proudly on the walls of his gas station. I began to collect pictures of boxers myself, and one of my favorites was a picture of a rather good looking Italian kid with a kind of brash look in his eyes. It was almost as though he was looking directly at me.

As I developed an affinity for the sport of boxing I became a student of the sport and, because of my Italian heritage, I gravitated towards following the careers of the great Italian American boxers. On the nights of televised fights, whether it would be Wednesday or Friday, my mother would cook one of her usual wonderful meals, and we all would watch the greats go toe to toe. Tony was the working man's fighter. He seemed to represent the blue collar laborer, the policeman, the milkman and the factory worker.

Tony would take ten punches in order to land one devastating blow. People began to follow this young, tough Italian kid out of Boston's North End, which was known as little Italy. The night that he knocked out Johnny Saxton to win the Welterweight Championship (right in his own neighborhood) Italian Americans throughout the country celebrated. He was representing all of them, the immigrants who came to this country to find the dream.

In 1977, I decided to establish the Italian American Boxing Hall of Fame. The first person that I contacted was Angelo Dundee, one of the greatest trainers of all time. I asked him who I could recruit to make calls to boxers around the country. Without hesitation, Angelo recommended that I contact three people: Tony, Carmen Basilio and Joey Giardello. Without the help of those three people, our dream would not have been realized. In September of that year 23 boxers were inducted. One year later we decided to expand to recognize all sports, and established the National Italian American Sports Hall of Fame.

Tony DeMarco is a member of that exclusive club. He is a member not only because he was a great fighter, but because he is a great man. Tony has remained humble and loyal to his friends and family. He never says no, and at a moments notice will be at an event to help out. I asked Tony to help us start a Massachusetts chapter of the National Italian American Sports Hall of Fame. Tony worked tirelessly to get this off the ground and, because of him, the Massachusetts chapter is flourishing. He was able to recruit some great businessmen and leaders in the Commonwealth, some of whom are still on the National Board of Directors to this day.

I am not going to get into the particulars of Tony's career. You are going to get a glimpse of that in the following pages. The only thing that I am going to say is that his epic battles with Carmen Basilio are much more than two great boxing matches. Both fights reflect the determination of two men that represented my culture and my heritage. Tony DeMarco was one of those two men, and Tony DeMarco in my eyes will always be the Champion.

George Randazzo, chairman and founder,
National Italian American Sports Hall of Fame

Introduction

As a little kid growing up in a very Italian neighborhood in Lawrence, Massachusetts, a mill city about thirty miles north of Boston, I remember my father as well as my grandfather watching the "Gillette Cavalcade of Sports" on Friday nights. Dad and Nanno actively followed the careers of the great Italian boxers representing Italian Americans across the country.

Willie Pep, Tony Galento, Joey Giardello and Jake LaMotta were a few of the boxing legends that they would root for. However, there were two that stood out above the rest. One was from the blue collar shoe manufacturing town of Brockton, and the other was from Boston's own North End. Both of these men became undisputed champions, and both were fiercely proud of their Italian heritage. Rocky Marciano went on to become one of the greatest heavyweights of all time retiring undefeated at 49-0, but this story is not about him. This is the life story of one of the most beloved and respected athletes in the annals of Boston sports, Tony DeMarco.

I remember my dad talking about the night that Tony knocked out Johnny Saxton to win the undisputed Welterweight Championship in his own neighborhood, right at the Boston Garden. I use the word "undisputed" because there was only one real champ in each weight division. Today you have many. My father spoke about the neighbors opening their windows and shouting in Italian *Campione del Mondo, Campione del Mondo;* "Champion of the World, Champion of the World." He talked about that victory for many years. As a Sicilian family we were so proud that a Sicilian had won the crown.

Many years later, long after my father and grandfather had passed on, I had the honor and pleasure to meet and become dear friends with Tony "Nardo" as he is affectionately known. There is a bit of dad in Tony, and there is a bit of Nanno. Every once in a while I see that wink, that nod, that mischievous smile that belonged only to a generation past of fathers and grandfathers that came from the old country.

Tony represents all of these men. The habits, the mannerisms, the quirkiness, it is all there. The difference between Nardo and all of the others is that his life was magnified by the fact that he was in the sporting limelight. Even though he became famous, Tony experienced the same joy and heartache over his life that I guess we all experience.

This is the story of a man that achieved greatness in his life, drifted a bit, and then overcame great obstacles to become a beloved figure in the boxing world as well as an ambassador for the sport and his heritage. This is the story of Nardo, a friend, a mentor, an inspiration.

Tom Zappala, author and talk show host

Round 1

Names

It is said that people in the limelight have many names. This is especially true for politicians, popular entertainers, and athletes. For example, the late, great, Frank Sinatra was called "The Crooner," "Old Blue Eyes," "The Leader of the Pack" and "The Chairman of the Board," just to name a few. As I rose through the ranks as a boxer, the same thing happened to me.

The name on my birth certificate is Leonardo Liotta. Born and raised on Fleet Street in Boston's historic North End, I thrived in that bustling Italian district. The neighborhood kids called me "Chubby" for most of my teen years. In school I was known as Len, Lenny, Leonard, and Leonardo. When I became a professional boxer, I fought under the name Tony DeMarco, sometimes shortened to TD, and eventually I became known as Champ.

One of my first professional nicknames came from Dave Egan, a columnist for the now defunct *Boston Herald American*. He dubbed me "The Flame and Fury of Fleet Street."

Over the course of my career, I ended up with even more names than Sinatra. The sportswriters all had their own nickname for me. To John Gillooly I was "Mr. Excitement" or "TD Two-Duked." Bud Collins found me to be "Short, Dark, and Harmful." Ed Fried called me "The Marciano of the Welterweights." To Larry Claflin I was "The Left Hooker."

Dave Gordon came up with three names for me: "The North End Exterminator," "TKO DeMarco," and "The Lion of Fleet Street." Dave Egan matched that with "TNT DeMarco," "The Little LaMotta," and "The Boston Battler."

Vic Johnson called me "The Pride of the North End," while Jerry

Nason dubbed me "The Skyrocket," and Tim Horgan named me "TD the Untamed Fury of Fleet Street."

But, my all-time favorite is my family nickname "Nardo" because, after all this time, I am still the Leonardo Liotta who grew up on Fleet Street in the Italian section of Boston and who ran home to dinner when my mother called out "Naaardo."

At this point not many people know me as Leonardo Liotta or call me Nardo. I have been Tony DeMarco for so long to so many people. How did I become Tony DeMarco? Stick around – that story will come a little later. If you were to walk through the streets of my old neighborhood with me today you would see that everyone knows me as "Champ."

I earned that name on the evening of April 1, 1955. Even though I had seven years as a professional boxer under my belt, I was only twenty-three years old. Little did I know what was in store for me in the years to come: the fame, the high life, but also the personal losses that would be so difficult.

On that night I was focused on one thing and one thing only – winning the Welterweight Championship. I wanted to win not just for myself, but for my family, my friends, my neighborhood, my city, and all who supported me along the way.

Nardo

The North End of Boston was a close-knit neighborhood. Neighbors were like family members and we all looked out for each other. As a kid, I was usually out playing with my chums when I was not in school. My mother, Giacomina, would have to shout loudly from the first floor of 13 Fleet Street so I could hear her, because I was usually a couple of blocks away at the corner of North and Fleet Streets. "Naaardo", "Naaardo" would echo through the neighborhood as she called me to come home for dinner.

Sometimes I was nowhere to be found as I would be off with my buddies Sal and Vito, the Venezia twins. Quite often, when Mom called for me, Sal and Vito's mother Maria would call out from her living room window to let my mother know she had cooked me dinner before I took off with her twins.

It was tradition in my family to wait for my father to come home from work and then eat dinner together. This was difficult for us kids since my father worked long hours at his cobbler shop and got home between seven and ten in the evening. We would be allowed to pick on a little fruit while eagerly waiting for Pa, but out of respect for the head of the household, we were never allowed to eat before him. No wonder I wandered off to Sal and Vito's for dinner now and then.

Mom and Pa were blessed with five children. The eldest, Leonardo, died of diphtheria shortly before I was born. My other siblings were Josephine, who became the eldest, Mary who was a year younger than I, and Andrew who we nicknamed Gary.

This probably sounds very strange, but ever since I was little, I always felt that I might be the reincarnation of my older brother Leonardo. I guess this is because I carry his name.

Why would my parents name two children the same name? Well, Leonardo was an important name in Pa's family because it was my grandfather's name. My father, Vincenzo Liotta, had two sisters and one brother. They all married and had families, and all named their sons Leonardo.

Aunt Ann's son Leonardo Nuciforo was a little older than me, but we were chums. We hung out together with the rest of the kids from Fleet Street. My second cousin Leonardo Bono was much older and was more the intellectual type. He always impressed me with his love of life.

Uncle Luigi's son, Leonardo Liotta, worked for my father in his shoe repair shop. He was a good worker and Pa was very proud of him. During World War II, Leonardo joined the U.S. Navy and Pa proudly hung a picture of his nephew in uniform in the shop. When he was younger, he was a scrappy kid who fought in the amateurs. He was a good boxer and had quite a few victories under his belt. This cousin later moved to Florida and became a golfer.

I was closest to Aunt Camellia's son, cousin Leonardo Rossi who had a reputation as a tough street fighter. He lived just around the corner so I saw him quite often. We thought a lot of each other and occasionally he would give me a nickel or a dime which I would spend at the candy store.

You can see the name Leonardo was a very popular name in my family.

Mio Padre Il Mio Eroe

My Father Is My Hero

Vincenzo was just a teenager when he came to America with his parents and siblings at the turn of the twentieth century. They left their home in Sciacca, Sicily for the chance of a better life in New York. After a short time, the family moved to Massachusetts and settled in Boston's North End. This section of the city was home to immigrants from southern Italy and the island of Sicily, so they were able to become part of the community very quickly.

As might be expected of a recent immigrant, my father held tightly to his Sicilian traditions. Marriage for him was not an option until his two sisters, Annie and Camellia were married and provided for. As a young man, his first priority was to become established in business so he could help support the family.

Although he was young, Vincenzo was a good cobbler, and he soon became the proud proprietor of the Trinity Cobbler Shop located on Dartmouth Street near the Copley Plaza Hotel. That area is filled with upscale fashionable stores today, but at the time it was a working class neighborhood.

Pa worked hard to make his shop a success. After Camellia and Annie were married it was finally Vincenzo's turn. He returned to Sicily to find his bride and the pretty Giacomina Ragusa caught his eye. He fell in love and courted Giacomina until she agreed to marry. After marrying in Sicily they returned to Boston to start a family.

Once back in Boston, with a growing family to support, Pa worked even harder at his shop. He put in long hours and worked six and a half days a week. Because most of his customers spoke English, Pa quickly learned to speak the language rather well.

I started helping out at the shop in 1943, when I was about eleven years old. I worked on the weekends during the school year and during the summer I worked every day. When Pa didn't need help because business was slow, I worked as a newsboy. My route started at the shop and went through the surrounding Back Bay neighborhood. I sold newspapers all along the way but always spent most of my time near the restaurants

That's me in the second row. This is the caption that was printed in the newspaper:
"Strike's Over. North End children face the camera outside Michelangelo School today
before returning to classes to end a two-day strike. Grievances which the pupils claimed
were partly responsible for their walkout were under investigation."

because I sold a lot more papers there.

As I got a few years older, my father taught me how to repair shoes. I enjoyed the work because it was a great opportunity to meet interesting people. The streets surrounding the shop were full of friendly faces and Pa's shop was always busy.

But it was not in the cards for me to become a cobbler. When I was fourteen, David Finkelstein bought the entire block-long building where Pa's shop was located. He gave all of the business owners notice to vacate when their leases expired. He then proceeded to paint the windows green in all of the empty shops and topped each window with a shamrock. This was his way of promoting a bar he had purchased along with the block.

Although my father's lease had not expired and his shop was still open, his business started to drop off dramatically because the rest of the block was boarded up. Sadly, after thirty years at his shop, Pa had to close up for good. He was not able to find another location in the area for his shop, so he sold all of his equipment and looked for another job. At sixty-two years old he was put in the position of starting all over again.

The barber shop on the same block was owned by Pa's friend, Sal Pizza. Luckily he was able to find a new location for the barber shop and he offered Pa the opportunity to run a shoeshine concession inside his shop. My father made the most of this new business opportunity and was very happy to be working alongside his friends.

The Early Years

Growing up in an Italian neighborhood, my childhood was really no different than most city kids. We grew up on the streets of Boston, played together, fought together and created havoc together in the neighborhood, on the streets and, yes, at school.

One of my best friends in Junior High School was Ronnie Cassesso. He and I were known for creating a few headaches for the teachers in our school on a fairly regular basis. One day Ronnie and I, along with another buddy Joe "Black" Lamattina, decided the entire school should go on strike because our lunch break was not long enough. I was about thirteen years old and a student at the Michelangelo Junior High School, which didn't have a cafeteria. At lunchtime we were dismissed for a forty-five minute recess. Students would walk home for lunch and then return to school for the afternoon session. We thought that the forty-five minute break didn't give us enough time to walk home, eat lunch, and to get back to school in time.

The strike started first thing the very next morning. We all marched with signs and protested loudly. The students who didn't march and yell were too few in number to make any difference. We marched back and forth in front of the school all morning long. The strike quickly became a media event. Reporters from the Boston papers showed up, as well as reporters from *Life* and *Time* magazines. We were interviewed and pho-tographs were taken.

School administrators were quick to schedule a meeting with us, and

The Boys Club basketball team. That's me in the middle behind the guy holding the ball.

we appointed our friend Joe Black as spokesperson. Joe not only arranged to meet with the school's principal, but also with politicians from the city and state. The meeting took place in the school's auditorium. When all were present, Joe Black stepped up to microphone and spoke on the behalf of the students, saying, "Even if a person was as swift as a rabbit circling a dog track, we wouldn't have enough time to reasonably eat properly."

Joe requested that students be given an additional thirty minutes for their lunch break. It was the politicians, not the principal, who made the final decision. After they reviewed and discussed all the options, they decided to extend the break time by fifteen minutes. Students would now get a full hour for their lunch break. We were all satisfied with the decision and celebrated our victory. Little did I know that for me personally this would be the first of many victories. It was also pretty neat to get our picture in the paper.

My First Love: Boxing

I helped support my family by shoveling snow, delivering newspapers and shining shoes. Although I enjoyed all of my part-time jobs I didn't want to do any of them for an extended period. It was around this time that I started to get interested in the sport of boxing.

Most of the newsboys belonged to the Boston Club, a boys club run by the Burroughs Newsboy Foundation. It was established by Harry Burroughs, a Russian immigrant who started out in America working as a newsboy. After attending Suffolk Law School, Harry became very successful in the legal field. This allowed him to develop a club to help working children, among other philanthropic endeavors. Membership was only fifty cents a year. All city boys were welcome to join, even if they did not work as a newsboy. There were lots of activities geared toward teaching inner-city boys new skills such as music, arts and crafts, and sports.

Boys were encouraged to take leadership roles in the club. There were elections every year for club governor, mayor, and councilor. One of my chums from "the corner" Sammy Farinella, was so popular he was elected as the club's mayor for several terms.

Of all the sports activities at the club, I was most interested in learning boxing. Once I mastered the basic techniques, I fought as an amateur in Boston's Park Department League as well as the club, and word started to get around that I was a good boxer. I guess that I was one of those kids who had some natural talent.

***

At twelve years of age, weighing in at ninety-five pounds soaking wet, I entered the ring to compete in the three-night Greater Boston Boys Club Championship Tournament. On the first night I flattened my opponent in the first round. The second night was a repeat of the first. On the third night, the match lasted all of two rounds. My opponent passed out before the third round. The crowd went wild. All of my chums from the North End came to see me fight. They bragged about being there, and word of my victory spread throughout the North End. This victory gave me my first important championship win. I was on my way.

Sweet as Sugar

Frankie "Biffo" Waters, an old-time respected boxer, decided to take in interest in me. "So, you want to be a professional fighter, huh? I'll tell you what," he said, "I'm taking you to the Boston Garden to see the greatest fighter ever!" I was so excited all I could say was "Wow!" What a great opportunity. I was thirteen years old and about to see a professional fight for the first time.

Biffo was taking me to see Sugar Ray Robinson, the future welterweight champion of the world. He was going to fight Vic Dellicurti, a tough welterweight contender from Detroit, on December 4, 1945. I was so thrilled I never even thought to ask how Biffo happened to get his hands on an extra fight ticket which cost $1.25. That night, he "tipped" the right person and we ended up sitting at ringside.

The evening was thrilling for me as I could see Sugar Ray Robinson's style of boxing up close. With masterful footwork and his unique way of bouncing off the ropes, Sugar Ray hit Dellicurti with combinations literally at will. It seemed like Robinson was just looking for a ten-round workout without pressuring his opponent. It was no surprise that Sugar Ray was declared the winner, and no surprise to me when Sugar Ray won the welterweight title a year later.

There was even more excitement to come after the main event that night. On the same card was a particularly intense local grudge match between Vincent Yima Troy from Boston's North End, and Johnny Bates, a favorite from Boston's West End. Both neighborhoods were home to blue collar families living in tenements, but the West End was multi-cultural while the North End was predominately Italian.

The contest was savage from the start, with the two fighters matching each other punch for punch, and knockdown for knockdown. It was a toe-to-toe battle until the final bell sounded, and both boxers anxiously awaited the judges' decision. It seemed like it took forever, but the judges finally came in with a split decision.

That left it up to the referee to raise the winner's hand. It was the man in the dark trunks, Vincent Yima Troy. The North Enders in The Garden that night were ecstatic. It had been a spectacular match, and symbolic of the rivalry between the two Boston neighborhoods. Both factions were ready to rumble after the fight, but in the end all they did was a little name calling back and forth. That night I told Biffo, that I too would someday fight in this very same arena. Little did I know that not only would my prediction ring true, but that the stakes would be for the World Championship.

Victorious in Charlestown

By the time I was thirteen I had bulked up to one hundred and fifteen pounds. That year the Burroughs Newsboys Club challenged the Charlestown Boys Club to a boxing match. Charlestown was known as the Irish section of Boston, so the matches between the two clubs would bring the classic Irish-Italian rivalry into the ring as the Burroughs Boxing team was made up of boys from the North End.

The night of the match, no Charlestown boy weighed in at the same weight as me. That meant every would-be fighter had a match except for me. I was determined to fight that night and pestered our coach, Larry Sullivan, to work something out for me. Mr. Sullivan was a teacher at Medford High School. In addition to running the boxing club at the Burroughs Foundation, he was also a basketball coach.

He spoke with the Charlestown trainer, Joe Ferrante, who was nicknamed "Honey Melody." Joe was originally from the North End and had been one of the youngest fighters ever to win a national boxing championship.

Melody came up with a young man who was wearing a U.S. Navy uniform. He was twenty years old to my thirteen, and he outweighed me by at least fifteen pounds. Coach Sullivan refused to let me fight him. I kept insisting on the challenge until Coach finally relented and agreed to the match. There was no way that I was going to disappoint my friends who had all shown up to see me fight.

I entered the ring with great confidence and a self-assured swagger. The sailor was taller than me and well-developed, with muscular arms and a solid body. I remember he had a tattoo on his hairy chest and one on his right arm. In comparison I must have looked like a grammar school kid with no body hair as of yet. This was not a psychological drawback for me as I was pretty cocky. I was hungry to fight and determined to win. I was a wild strong and good punching southpaw without any fears to hold me back.

The referee gave the instructions, the bell rang, and I proceeded to throw continuous punches throughout the first round, oblivious to the age and size of the sailor. The second round was the same as the first. In round three, I threw devastating lefts, and just as the sailor was about to collapse, the referee stopped the fight. The crowd went wild. The word quickly spread in Boston's fight circles that this little Italian kid could really box, and my reputation grew rapidly, especially in the North End. Looking back on it now, I can see that this fight really started me on my journey to become the Welterweight Champ.

Most of the boys from the North End won that night, including

Posing with the great Jack Dempsey. I'm on the right.

12

my little brother, Gary, who weighed in at seventy-five pounds. Several of my friends were victorious including Filippo Bentivegna and "Lobo" DeMarco. As we were leaving the Charlestown Boys Club, a frustrated Honey Melody told Coach to "Take those kids back to the North End. I don't care if I ever see them again."

Jack Dempsey

As a youngster, I definitely had my share of memorable experiences. Because of my activities with the Boys Club in Boston and the City Parks Department League, I had the opportunity to meet many famous sports figures. The celebrity who thrilled me the most was the legendary Jack Dempsey, the former Heavyweight Champion of the World.

Jack was of Irish-Scottish ancestry, a descendent of pioneers who settled in Manassa, Colorado. His career began with a series of pick-up fights out West during the early part of the twentieth century. Dempsey's fame grew rapidly as he won most of the fights, and when he arrived in the East he was well received by boxing fans. He had seventy-seven fights and won fifty of them by knockout.

Mr. Dempsey, as I referred to him, traveled throughout the country visiting Boys Clubs and speaking to the youthful athletes of America. When he appeared at the Burroughs Newsboys Club in Boston, I had the pleasure of meeting him. I was all of fourteen years old, but was pegged as the club's best boxer. Because of this, I was chosen, along with another boy, Frank DeMeno, to be in a photograph with Mr. Dempsey. I was thrilled. "The Champ" stood between us as we posed for the camera.

One day, not long after my meeting with Mr. Dempsey, I wandered along the main street of Boston's shopping district. I was walking along Washington Street past the big department stores like Raymond's, Jordan Marsh, R.H. Whites, Filene's, and Filene's Basement Store, when I came up to the Adam Hat Store which was wedged in between the big guys. Adam hats were very popular at that time when men wore fedoras instead of baseball caps to cover their heads. As I passed the store, I began to sing their radio jingle to myself, "I know a man that wears an Adam hat." I kept repeating the melody over and over again as I walked by the store, gazing at the window display. Then I stopped and stared. There I was, right there in the window, next to Jack Dempsey. Someone had decided to use the photo of Jack Dempsey, flanked by Frank DeMeno and me, as part of the window display. I stared at the picture for quite a while and made it a point to walk by the store many more times in the future, until they finally changed the window display.

That meeting with Jack Dempsey had a big influence on my boxing career. I was inspired by his success and vowed to work hard so I, too, could be a champion one day.

Round 2

Tony DeMarco

It was now time to begin my journey as an amateur. There was, however, a little problem with this plan. The legal age to qualify for an amateur boxing license in Massachusetts was eighteen, but I was only fifteen years old. I had to figure out how to prove that I was old enough to qualify.

I found one of the boys from Fleet Street who was willing to help me out. Tony "Lobo" DeMarco was eighteen. We cooked up a plan for Lobo to go to Sacred Heart Church and ask Father Mario for a copy of his baptismal certificate to use as proof of age needed for employment. The certificate read "Antonio DeMarco, born September 16, 1929." Lobo gave me the certificate which I brought with me to the office of the State Boxing Commission. The local florist, Mr. Malvarosa, was kind enough to give me a ride. I passed the physical exam and got my amateur boxing license as Tony DeMarco, and that has been my name ever since.

Things got a bit more confusing when, several months later, Lobo decided that he wanted to box as an amateur. When I asked him what name he was going to use, he told me he planned to use his own. That would have meant trouble for me so I had to talk him out of it. Lobo spoke with some of the guys at the corner and ended up borrowing the name of his friend, Michael Termine. Michael also went to Father Mario for a copy of his baptismal certificate. Father Mario was happy to oblige and was pleased that the boys wanted to work. Later on, when Michael Termine decided to become a boxer as well, he had to use his older brother Marco's name. There we were...three boxers, using three different names, and keeping Father Mario happy. I was on my way.

Bobby "Ames" Agrippino approached me one day in 1947. At twenty-five, he was about ten years older than me. He lived three doors away on Fleet Street and, because he saw me fight several times, he was interested in my future as a boxer. Bobby was a short, skinny, expressive, convincing kind of guy. He had some experience as a corner man for Frankie "Ross" Toscano from the North End, who became a main event boxer in Miami, Florida. Frankie encouraged me to pursue my boxing goals. Both Frankie and Bobby impressed me with their outgoing personalities, and I wanted to impress them with my Boys Club victories.

I told them about my achievements boxing with the Boston Parks Department under the supervision of Michael Nazzaro, Sr. Mike was dedicated to the Boys Club and its philosophy of helping youngsters develop strong minds and bodies. He especially wanted to help kids from the North End.

I guess my record impressed Bobby and Frankie, because they both decided to work with me. Bobby became my first real manager as well as my mentor. I learned many of my life lessons from him. Frankie had learned from the school of hard knocks, and was a great fighter in his own right. He also mentored me, teaching me the intricacies of boxing techniques and strategies. Coogie McFarland was another important early influence. As my first trainer and cut man, Coogie helped me develop as both a boxer and as a young man. My first team was now in place. It was time to take it to the next level.

***

It was about this time that I started training at the New Garden Gym owned by Al Clemente and John Powers. Located just a stone's throw from Boston Garden, it was very close to my neighborhood and a convenient place to work out. Both Al and John took a special interest in the kids that frequented the place, and always treated us with respect. They were very sensitive to the limited finances of many of their young gym members, and were known to carry old dues on the books until the kids were able to pay what they owed.

At this point I was still boxing three round bouts and, on occasion, a five-rounder. I was getting frustrated with my slow progress toward becoming a true professional.

I had great sparring partners though. The main event boxers loved to spar with me, even though I was a lightweight at the time, and it really helped me progress as a boxer. I sparred with Alfred "Red" Priest, the New England middleweight champion. Priest was known for beating Tommy Sullivan, a strong fighter from the Irish South Boston neighborhood. They fought on December 17, 1946 to a sellout crowd at the Boston Garden, breaking the record for ticket sales.

Later on, in the early 1950s, I sparred with other well-known middleweights including Joe Rindone and Norman Hayes. Rindone was knocked out in the sixth round by Sugar Ray Robinson on October 16, 1950, in Boston. Hayes was known for his fights with tough guys like Jake LaMotta, Robert Villemain, Joey DeJohn, and Paul Pender, the local middleweight champion. Hayes and Pender had two terrific ten round brawls in Boston. On December 11, 1950, Hayes beat Pender in ten rounds. On January 8, 1951, Pender beat Hayes by a knockout in the seventh round.

The Amateurs

Now that I had my amateur boxing license, and had been training at the New Garden Gym, it was time to take the next step and set up my first amateur fight. The match would be against Richard Cole of Lynn. I was still only fifteen years old when I began my career with a second round knockout victory at the old Boston Arena.

My early years in the ring had many people taking notice of my skills. Of my twelve amateur fights I won ten. There was a TKO against Anthony Messina of Brockton, where I was cut but won by decision, and nine wins by KO's. After winning seven fights in a row, I fought Al White of Framingham and won by decision. Three more KO wins, and I had made it to the semi-finals for the New England Amateur Championship at the Boston Arena. There I fought George Araujo from Providence, Rhode Island in an elimination bout and lost by decision. Unfortunately I was out of the running for the Amateur Championship that year, but overall, I was pleased with the progress I was making.

Training with the guys at the New Garden Gym. I'm second from right.

Later on, as a professional, George Araujo fought the best of the world contenders and beat them all. He held the New England Professional Lightweight Championship title, but when he competed for the undisputed Lightweight Championship title, he lost to Jimmy Carter in an excellent fight that lasted thirteen rounds. Years later, when I faced Araujo as a professional in a highly touted contest at Fenway Park, I knocked him out in the fifth round.

Haverhill

There were many memorable fights during my amateur career, but after all these years, one night really stands out in my mind. I was scheduled to fight at Haverhill City Hall but I didn't know how I was going to get there. My trainer Coogie McFarland and my corner man Frankie Campbell were both out of town, and I had to travel about thirty miles north of Boston to get to the fight. My manager, Bobby Agrippino, took charge of my corner, along with the responsibility of getting me to Haverhill. Bobby contacted Mr. Malvarosa, the florist, who once again came to the rescue, and drove us to the fight.

One of the promising young boxers fighting in the heavyweight division that night was Peter Fuller, the grandson of the former Massachusetts governor, Alvin Tufts Fuller. Outgoing and popular, Peter kept himself in great fighting condition and promoters were happy to help advance his career.

I weighed in at 125 pounds that night, and was matched up with another up-and-coming fighter who had ventured to Haverhill. I knocked him out in the middle of the first round. What a thrill!

The best fighter that evening was going to win a large trophy, and I wanted to come home with that trophy. Usually I sold my amateur trophies back to the promoters for $10 or $15 which would give me a bit of extra spending money. Added to the money I earned from my odd jobs, I would be able to pay my gym dues, help with the family expenses, and have enough left to go see two or three movies a week. This trophy was big and beautiful though, and I really wanted to win it.

There was another boxer who had been left without an opponent that evening in Haverhill. I was offered the opportunity to fight him and decided to go for it. I figured this would help my chances of winning the trophy. If I had two fights and won both, I would surely be named the best boxer of the evening.

In that second fight, I quickly disposed of the other boxer with a left hook for my second win of the evening. As I sat in the dressing room waiting for the other bouts to end, Bobby found out that a featherweight boxer had canceled, and the promoters wanted to know if I would take his place. When Bobby asked if I was interested, I jumped at the chance to fight again. If I won three bouts, I would definitely go home with that trophy.

There I was back in the ring. The fans went absolutely wild because I was about to start my third fight of the evening. The first round ended with me building my confidence. In the middle of the second round, I hit my opponent with a left hook and knocked him out. I assured myself that the Outstanding Fighter trophy would be mine to take home.

There was, however, a development that I did not anticipate. Peter Fuller was not scheduled to fight until the last bout of the evening. His opponent was no match to Peter in ability, but he did manage to stay the full three rounds in a very boring match. Fans started to walk out before the decision was announced. As they passed me in the back of the hall where I was waiting, they congratulated me on my three victories.

After Peter's victory was announced, it was time for the Outstanding Fighter Award presentation. I was shocked when the ring announcer called Peter Fuller's name and awarded him the trophy. I was so disappointed. After winning three fights, I was sure the trophy would be mine, but instead I was awarded a beautiful Emerson watch. I decided to keep it rather than selling it back to the promoters. The next day, the Haverhill newspaper had a spectacular headline about my three victories and my promising career. I still have the clippings and fond memories of that exciting evening in Haverhill. Little did I realize, that many years later the City of Haverhill would make up for the slight by presenting me with a plaque that read: "Outstanding Fighter Award." I accepted that award with pride when I was 75 years old.

About a month after the Haverhill tournament, I was scheduled to fight at Haverhill City Hall again. That night I faced a boy from South Boston named John Quinn and proceeded to KO him in the fourth round. The Haverhill newspaper again reported my victory with a big story that ran with the headline "DeMarco Steals City Hall Show Again," in large bold print. The prize that evening was a small trophy which I was happy to sell back to the fight promoter for $10.

Southpaw No More

Through Coogie, I met a guy named Jimmy Doyle, a New Yorker working out of Canada. His working interest was a fighter from Montreal named Johnny Greco. A contender for the welterweight championship, Greco was in Boston to fight at the Garden against Ralph "The Ripper" Zannelli of Providence. The fight went ten exciting rounds and Ralph won by a unanimous decision.

Coogie worked in Ralph's corner as a cut man. After the fight, he and Jimmy Doyle got together to share fight stories which included some of my amateur fights. I was soon scheduled for my next amateur fight in Lynn, just north of Boston, and Doyle decided to stick around to watch me fight. For this Lynn fight, I was matched with a U.S. Marine Corps champion in the featherweight division. The marine was tall and wiry and tipped the scale at 128 pounds, as did I. In the middle of the first round, I had him up against the ropes and hit him with a barrage of rights and lefts before I knocked him out with a left hook. That ended the match. Doyle was astonished, not only by the knockout, but also by the style of knockout.

After the fight, Jimmy had only one suggestion. He said that the barrage of the type I had thrown followed by such a powerful left-handed punch indicated that I should become a right-handed fighter, and this would give me an edge. In order to make the switch I would need to train myself to lead or jab with my left and punch with my right which would be kept close to my body. This would be a difficult feat to accomplish as I was used to doing the exact opposite.

I decided to follow Jimmy's advice and, from that point on in my career, trained as a converted "southpaw." To help me make the transition Bobby, and trainer Frank MacFallen, decided to tie my right arm behind my back while I trained. They did this for three days straight. All I could do was jab and hook with my left hand. I worked at this continuously and eventually got the knack of it. The result was that my left hook became a dynamite punch, which was an important factor in my successful boxing career.

The Kid training in leather boots.

Round 3

Tony DeMarco "Pro"

I was sixteen, and my managers decided that if I turned professional, I could start making some money. The prize for a four round fight was $50 and it jumped to $75 for six rounds. Because I was just starting out, I had to pay $15 for my boxing license and $10 for a cardiogram. Each time I fought I had to pay $2 for a good steak before the fight, $5 for transportation, and $5 for a third corner man. We would enjoy a celebratory pizza, and then the rest of the purse would go toward my gym fees. Luckily my managers picked up all the expenses and that way I could pocket the purse. I would keep $5 or $10 for spending money until my next fight, and give the rest to my mother to help with our family expenses. The bouts were held about a month apart, depending on how Coogie felt about my potential opponents. As far as he was concerned all comers were welcome because, to quote his favorite expression, they were all "a bunch of spittoon bums."

We finally decided I should take the plunge into professional boxing. I would be fighting as a lightweight. Because I was "the local kid," my first pro fight took place at the Boston Garden. My opponent was another local boxer, Meteor Jones. On October 21, 1948, in front of a crowd of about 8000 people, I stepped into the ring. Here I was, Tony DeMarco, fighting at the legendary Garden in front of my hometown fans.

That night I made quick work of Jones, knocking him out in the first round. I was sixteen years old and ready to take on the world. Three weeks later, in a rematch at the Salem Arena, I knocked out Meteor Jones again, this time in the second round. My professional career had begun, and I was 2-0.

The Wiseguys

Little did I know at the time that my trainer and corner man, Coogie McFarland, was quite the character. A heavyset guy known for his great sense of humor and colorful language, Coogie was well-known and well-liked by the "wiseguys."

The term "wiseguy" was used to describe individuals who were associated with the underworld. They were the soldiers who carried out the orders given by the men who controlled illegal activities throughout New England.

On a hot summer evening in 1949, my friend Anthony "Smeaky" Pasquale and I decided to head over to the Scollay Square Arcade for a little fun. Smeaky was five years older than me but we were the same weight, 132 pounds. He had just been discharged from the U.S. Army and we started to chum around together that summer. Scollay Square had been a recreation spot for servicemen during World War II, but by that time it had somewhat deteriorated. They still had a great arcade with a large collection of pinball machines, so Smeaky and I had a lot of fun competing to see who was the most talented with the ball and flippers that evening.

We had a great time at the arcade, and after a few hours we walked the half mile back to the North End, getting to my neighborhood just in the nick of time. I saw my twelve-year-old brother Gary out selling newspapers. He was at the Florentine Bar hoping to make a few sales to the patrons. Gary decided to stack some of his newspapers on a car parked nearby. Unfortunately, the car belonged to a street punk nicknamed Billy "The Bug," a low man on the wiseguy totem pole. The street corner by the Florentine was a regular hangout for many of the Boston wiseguys.

Out of nowhere, The Bug appeared and started to assault Gary for putting newspapers on his car. I immediately charged over to defend my brother and got involved in a confrontation with Billy. Smeaky, who was older and wiser, knew this was a no-win situation considering The Bug's profession.

Thankfully he held me back from inflicting an old fashioned beat down on Billy, and thankfully they all knew I was Coogie's protégée. Henry "Noyes" Selvitelli, an upper-level wiseguy intervened. He made Billy apologize to Gary, who then continued on with his paper route. I

Training with my biggest fan, my father.

stayed behind and accepted the apology extended to me but, before leaving, I just couldn't resist saying to The Bug, "Any time you want to battle, I'll be ready."

Gary

My little brother Andrew, nicknamed Gary, was a good athlete and even played baseball with the older guys from time to time. Like me, Gary got into boxing and fought with the Boston Parks Department. He was a good boxer. Mike Nazzaro thought Gary had the talent to pursue the sport, and spent a lot of time working with him.

Even though Gary was five years younger than me, we were very close. He was not just a brother to me; he was my friend. I remember a few times when we would get into scuffles with other kids from the neighborhood.

My brother, my best friend.

Gary would always take on the younger one, and I would take on the older one. We made a good team.

As kids, Gary and I sold newspapers together. We would work the restaurant and bar circuit because it was good business for us. Gary sang while selling his papers and frequently received tips. I still remember one incident with a Boston cop. Gary and I went into a North End restaurant to sell papers. A policeman approached us and accused me of pulling the fire alarm on the corner of Parmenter and Hanover Streets. I denied the charge, explaining to the officer that my brother and I had been busy selling papers as usual at the local Hanover Street establishments.

Of course the policeman didn't believe me. He insisted that I confess to setting off the fire alarm. I told him that I was innocent of the charge but the policeman still didn't believe me. I was taken to the closest North

End police station on North Street. Once we were inside, the policeman slapped me around as we walked up to the officer at the duty desk. When we were in front of the desk, the officer behind it asked me my name. I stood silent.

The duty officer then came across the desk and slapped me so hard that I almost fell to the floor. Thankfully another officer took me aside. He seemed to care about me, so I gave him my name and address. Word of my situation didn't take long to reach my father. Within minutes Pa and Gary arrived at the police station and although he was very young, Gary came running in ready to take on the world. Pa reasoned with the police officers and talked them into releasing me.

We left the station and walked home to Fleet Street. "Nardo" my father began, "I believe what your brother told me. I believe that you are innocent of the charge, so I think you should go out and play and forget about all of this." Vincenzo was the type of father who understood things better than we did. Once we were out of the house, he took the rest of our papers and gave them to the neighbors.

Not too long after that, Gary became ill. At first my parents could not figure out what was wrong, but after some medical tests, it was determined that Gary was suffering from kidney disease. He was put on a regimen of different medications, but nothing seemed to help. Medical technology at the time was still in its infancy stages when it came to dealing with kidney disease. It was very difficult for the entire family to watch helplessly as Gary's condition worsened. My dear brother suffered for about a year, and passed away at the age of fourteen.

We never really got over the loss of Gary. To this day he is still fondly remembered by family and friends. I think about him every day. My biggest regret is that he never got the opportunity to be in my corner with me when I won the World Championship.

Training Outside of the Gym

As a kid, I got into a few scraps outside of the ring. These, of course, were through no fault of my own.

One evening, I was back on the corner in the North End hanging around Joe Christy's Luncheonette and chatting with my friends, Sal "Fernando" Cardone and Smeaky. We were very close, and always looked out for each other. On this occasion we saw three guys insulting some North End girls we knew. Naturally we had to defend their honor, so we proceeded to rough up the three punks pretty good. We disappeared before anyone saw us. After all, I couldn't afford to jeopardize my budding boxing career.

Another incident sticks out in my mind. I was a guest at the wedding of Fernando's sister, Rose. This was quite a lavish affair held at Boston's Hotel Kenmore. After the reception a couple of guys, who were also wedding guests, had a bit too much to drink and got a little carried away. I stepped in to try and get them under control. I was forced to straighten one guy out, and was about to do the same to the second one. My pal Vito Venezia intervened and calmly explained to the second guy that he should examine his behavior, or I would have to educate him. Both troublemakers got the hint, and ran off like a couple of deer.

After they disappeared, I discovered that my coat was ripped from the lapel pocket all the way down to the side pocket. I was a goner with Mom. It is interesting that I had just beat up two punks, but was more concerned about dealing with my mother over a ripped sport coat. The coat was bought with borrowed money which hadn't been paid back yet. I contacted a friend, Lou Bruno, who worked in a clothing factory as a stitcher. Thankfully, Lou was able to expertly repair the two-foot rip and didn't even charge me for his services. In later years, Lou later went on to become a pretty accomplished comedian and dance man.

Newark

One morning my friend Sardo Campo and I were sipping coffee at Joe Christy's Luncheonette when Bobby Agrippino came over. He told us that he had been talking to Coogie about how slow the boxing game had become in Boston, and they thought I should go where the boxing action was. That meant going to the New York City area, and hopefully getting the opportunity to fight at Madison Square Garden. Coogie had already spoken with New York promoter Willie Gilzenberg, the manager of Tony Galento. Willie assured him that if I moved to New York or New Jersey they could do business.

At this point in my career, I was 20-3 and climbing up the ladder. I had beaten some good boxers, but it was time to take on better competition.

After thinking everything over I decided the move would be good for my career. It would give me the opportunity to fight more often so I could make some decent money, but first I would need my father's approval. In an old fashioned Italian family like ours, out of respect, I would need to receive the permission and blessing of my father. Besides, I was still an underage kid. I finally got up the nerve and spoke with Pa. He gave me his blessing and I began to prepare for my trip to New Jersey.

The first thing I needed was a suitcase. Up to this point in my young life, the only bag I ever needed was the tote I used to carry equipment to my fights. Because my funds were limited, the only suitcase I could afford was a duffle bag from a local Army Navy store, so that's what I ended up with.

Even though I couldn't afford one, I also needed a suit. I borrowed some money and went to the legendary Filene's Basement, a Boston landmark that became famous for bargain prices on brand name clothing. With the $29 that I borrowed, I was able to get a great deal on a new suit. I already had socks, shoes, shirts, ties, shorts, a sweater, a hat and a jacket. It was a limited wardrobe but it got me through. When it was time to leave for New Jersey, I packed everything in my new duffle bag.

Before I took off, I got in touch with Dante DeChristoforo, an older friend who had always mentored and encouraged me. Dante had a cousin who lived in Newark and he told me how to look him up. When it was time to go, Dante and a few other friends had a farewell dinner party for me. They took me to Chinatown in Boston where I tasted Chinese food for the very first time. I really enjoyed my initiation to this type of cooking, and my final night out with the boys.

Dressed in my new suit, I boarded the train in Boston that would take me to Newark. Willie Gilzenberg was supposed to meet me at the Newark train station but he sent one of his associates, Nunzio Sica, to greet me instead. Nunzio brought me to Newark's Carlton Hotel. It wasn't a bad place and the rates were reasonable, but I couldn't afford the $5 a day room charge so I asked Nunzio to help me find someplace else to stay. After about a week at the Carlton, Nunzio found me a room located about a half mile away from where he lived. The room had a small bed, a small rack for clothing and a small sink. It was like living in a cold water flat which was something I was well accustomed to. The bathroom was in the corridor and shared by all the tenants on my floor but it had a shower and my room was heated, which were two big pluses for me.

Almost every night I ended up at Nunzio's and was treated to a good meal prepared by Mrs. Sica. After dinner we would watch television, and then I would take their pet Boxer for a long walk. That helped me learn the layout of the streets in their Newark suburb of North Arlington. Soon I was able to take my daily run in that area without getting lost. The route I ran every day took me through a local cemetery which I knew was not the best place for a workout, but it was the only place I had. One day a police cruiser followed me while I was shadow boxing during my sunrise run through the cemetery. I was focused on my training and hadn't noticed the company, so I really jumped when they honked the horn. I didn't appreciate their little joke, but in time I got to know the policemen who patrolled the beat. They were pretty good guys and were kind enough to keep an eye on me.

The Arena Gymnasium was right in the heart of Newark, at the corner of Broad and Market Streets. Nunzio was charged with taking me to the gym for my training sessions. The place was nothing special, certainly not the cleanest gym I had ever been in, and during the winter months I think it was one of the coldest buildings in New Jersey.

Through Nunzio I met a knowledgeable trainer and former fighter, Red Lambers. He was hired by Willlie Gilzenberg to watch over me during my training. Red had worked with George Araujo when he was in the area. George and I had a history as sparring partners well before our fights. Although we started together, Araujo was a main-eventer in those days and I was still struggling with six and eight round fights.

Another boxer I met was Tippy Larkin, the 1946 World Junior Welterweight Champion. Larkin, whose real name was Antonio Pilleteri, was known as the "Garfield Gunner" because he was from Garfield, New Jersey. Tippy was the real deal. In those days, it was easier to get your foot in the door in business, sports, and entertainment if you had an Anglo-sounding name. Tippy, like many other people with Italian names, found this to be true.

I was Tippy's sparring partner as he prepared for his comeback trail from a tough loss. He had sprained his ankle during his last fight with Joey Lupo, and as a result the fight was stopped in the sixth round. While we trained together at Greenwood Lake, Angelo Pucci worked on the ankle so Tippy could continue on. Pucci was a very good trainer and had managed many fighters including George Araujo, who I would eventually meet in the ring again.

My first fight in New Jersey was at the Laurel Garden in Newark. It was only a preliminary bout but it was very important to me because I needed to show Newark that I had the potential to become a main-eventer. Even though Nunzio's brother Jimmy "Wild" Sica was working in my corner as a cut man that night, I sorely missed the support I was accustomed to in Boston, where all my friends would show up to cheer me on.

Frankly, moral support is an important factor in sports and very helpful as you try to prove yourself. I was feeling a little down and very alone as I waited for my turn to climb into the ring. Just when I was feeling pretty low Dante's cousin, Pat Villanova, came up and introduced himself. We started talking about Dante and all of our mutual friends in Boston who wished they could be there to support me. This was enough of a catalyst to get me out of my pre-fight funk, and I went on to knock out my opponent, Stanley Hilliard. It was November 27, 1951. That night also marked the beginning of a great friendship with Pat.

I ended up spending a lot of time with Pat while I was in Newark. Besides meeting his family, I was introduced to a lot of guys from great organizations like the West End Club and the Paramount Club. I spent quite a bit of time hanging out at these clubs and, more often than not, ate dinner with Pat's parents. Newark became a little more comfortable for me because Pat and the guys in Newark had become my friends. It was almost like being back in Boston. With their support, I went for it, barnstorming all over New Jersey and New York, boxing in Newark, Trenton, Manhattan, and Brooklyn. My record by this time was 26-3. I was gaining momentum and getting better at my craft.

On February 26, 1952, I beat Abdul Ali with a knockout punch in the second round of what was supposed to be a six round fight. A few days later while I was working out at the gym, Willie Gilzenberg called to ask me if I would be interested in filling in for Tony Pellone, a good welterweight who could not fight because of an eye injury. The fight was to take place in Brooklyn and the opponent would be Jackie O'Brien, a tough boxer who had been around awhile. Willie thought the match would be a good career move for me.

I had been at the gym only one day since my last fight, but the match was worth $380 and 17% of the gate, so it was very tempting. The fight would be televised locally, and that was the reason for the big gate. This would be a very big opportunity for me, but I couldn't help but feel that I was being used. Why? First, and foremost, O'Brien was a welterweight and I was still fighting as a lightweight. Second, if your goal is to build up a fighter, you do not bring him into the ring to fight after a one-day training period. I was frustrated that Willie would even consider such a bout. He was just thinking about his own payday and not looking out for my best interests. I hung up on Willie and went back to my workout.

All during that workout, I kept thinking about the $380 purse plus the 17% of the gate for local television rights. It was just too much money to pass up in those days. After thinking it over, I decided that I would use the winnings to pay off some loans and finally send some serious money home. Even though I thought Willie was taking advantage of me, I called him back and accepted the last minute match against O'Brien.

I won the fight in an eight-round unanimous decision on March 1, 1952. I was so thrilled that I called my parents and my sisters Josephine and Mary. I proudly told them that they could soon expect a few hundred dollars from me in the mail.

The next day I went to Willie's promotions office at the South Orange Avenue Rose Bowl to collect my winnings. Willie was also involved in the wrestling business, and this is where the matches were held. As a matter of fact, one of the wrestlers in his stable was "Two Ton" Tony Galento who had lost the Heavyweight Championship to the great Joe Louis by a knockout.

Willie talked to me about the reality of the money situation. He detailed all of the expenses from my arrival in Newark to the present. As we talked, the $650 purse (pay plus percentage of the gate) got smaller and smaller. Gilzenberg subtracted all expenses from the time that I checked into the Carlton Hotel to every stick of chewing gum that was bought for me. Needless to say, after I sent the money I promised to my family, I was right back to my "short money" position.

After just one more fight I decided to return home, because I was both homesick and strapped for cash. My last fight in Newark took place on March 6, 1952, at the Laurel Garden against "Puggy" Brown. The night before, I came down with a very bad cold but I was determined to fight anyway. I wanted to go home to Boston but needed some money, so there was no way I was going to let a cold keep me from fighting.

I had been developing a New Jersey following, and was also pleasantly surprised when friends from Boston drove down to watch the fight. One of my Newark friends, who owned a dry cleaning shop in North Arlington, came to the fight with his wife and two sons. They sat in the fifth row ringside and cheered as I threw the final punch before the fight was stopped. I connected with a left hook that jarred Puggy's mouthpiece and actually sent it flying right to the fifth row where my friends were sitting. They were thrilled with their new souvenir.

The next day Nunzio stopped by my apartment along with Fernando Cardone and Sonny DeLeo, who had come from Boston to take me home. I was anxious to return to my roots although I would miss my New Jersey friends. Willie Gilzenberg however, was not one of them. In my opinion, Willie was only interested in his own financial gain, and never really looked out for me. I couldn't wait to get home to my friends and family in the North End.

***

According to Coogie things were still slow in the Boston boxing world. As a result, I began hanging around the North End and quickly became part of the well-entrenched street corner society. I became a regular at some of the storefront "private clubs" in the neighborhood. At this point I actually started to seriously think about quitting the ring for a while so I could get a steady job with a regular income.

That notion did not last very long. I soon got a call from Bobby Agrippino who told me I could fight in a couple of weeks in Montreal. Apparently Coogie had already made the arrangements with Eddie Quinn, a former Boston promoter now working out of that area. I reluctantly accepted the offer even though I would have only two weeks to train. I felt like I was destined to be a last minute substitute boxer.

I was matched up against Brian Kelly, a tough little guy from Niagara Falls. Eddie Quinn had a personal interest in Brian and another boxer from the same area, Gene Poirer. That night I lost to Brian Kelly in an eight-round decision.

Coogie surprised me by arranging a match only two weeks later with Gene Poirer, Quinn's other protégé. Gene was a good boxer and almost as tough as Brian Kelly. The decision was very much the same. I lost in eight rounds. After the fight Coogie paid me off under the light of a two-watt bulb. The money was the same as the wattage, very low. The next day I was picked up by a chauffer driven limousine and taken back to New York City along with Coogie, Bobby, Eddie Quinn and his companion, burlesque queen Lili St. Cyr. That was not enough to cheer me up. I had lost two fights in a row. In all honesty, it was not because the opponents were better, but because I was given absolutely no direction.

Back in Boston, I began to think about my future. It was time to make some decisions about my career. Coogie was starting to hinder my boxing career by not putting in the effort I thought was necessary for me to pursue my dreams. I finally came to the conclusion that it was time to replace him. Bobby Agrippino wasn't as experienced as Coogie, but he had become a close friend and having an older person with boxing knowledge in my corner was extremely important. To make matters worse, I found out that Willie Gilzenberg and Nunzio Sica still had the contract I signed with them when I was nineteen years old. They were trying to hold me to the contract but, because of my age when I signed, I was not legally bound by it. In spite of this, I was afraid of being blackballed if I didn't honor the contract. Besides that, there is one other point that I forgot to mention. Nunzio Sica was part of the largest crime family in New Jersey.

Feeling caught between a rock and a hard place, I decided to fight fire with fire. I approached Phil Buccola, an influential man who was well-known in boxing circles throughout the United States and Italy. Phil also happened to be head of the New England mob. He had an interest in fighters like Dulio Spagnulo, a heavyweight from Italy. Buccola hoped Spagnulo would become the next heavyweight champion but things didn't work out the way Phil planned. A mediocre fighter, Spagnulo was outmatched and never materialized as a contender. He did win several fights in the States but Spagnulo returned to Italy clearly understanding that he could not compete.

Phil Buccola was about to begin negotiations with Nunzio Sica regarding my contract when he was called back to Italy for business reasons. Before leaving for Italy he got in touch with Dick Hogan and Johnny Buckley. Dick was his nephew through marriage who had served in the army and was also a boxer. Johnny was a boxing promoter and manager. Phil left instructions with them to negotiate with the boys from New Jersey and resolve my contract. Nunzio and Buckley discussed the disposition of my contract for quite some time and could not come up with an equitable solution. To me it seemed like Buckley didn't want to pay the $1,000 plus asking price of the contract. I was stuck in boxing limbo, and because of this dilemma, I decided to pack it in. It was time for me to take some time off, clear my head, and see if I really wanted to continue on with my boxing career.

Back home with Pa.

Round 4

California

One of my buddies, Barney Lanci, suggested that a bunch of us make a cross-country trip to California. Barney was a lot of fun and very sharp, with a mind that was always going a mile-a-minute concocting crazy schemes. This idea came up at the perfect time for me. It would be an opportunity to enjoy the West Coast, and possibly make some money boxing under an assumed name, since I would be far enough away from New Jersey where I had a signed contract. Actually, as Tony DeMarco I was already boxing under an assumed name, so all I would need was a different assumed name. Barney and the guys loved this plan so we got serious about mapping out our trip.

Jerry Tecce, another North End pal, decided to come with us to California. He was the brother of Boston restaurateur Joe Tecce who owned Joe Tecce's Italian restaurant, one of the more famous restaurants in the city of Boston. Berrio Gizzi, another pal, also decided to get in on the fun. A talented artist, Berrio enjoyed sitting in the coffee shop and sketching the patrons. When he ran out of paper, he would draw right on the table. On a couple of occasions his subjects tried to take the table home with them so they could keep his drawing. One of his better sketches was of the movie star Lana Turner. Berrio had a plan to track down Turner in California, show her the sketch, and see if she would put in a good word for him out there.

The final member of our group was Irving Stein, a friend of Barney Lanci's. Irving decided to chip in with the driving and figured he could stay with relatives and friends once we got to the West Coast. Barney knew Irving from the G&G Delicatessen in Mattapan, which at the time was

37

one of Boston's predominately Jewish neighborhoods. The restaurant was a popular late night gathering place for entertainers, musicians, and sports figures. Barney loved the environment and the food. We went to the G&G with Barney quite a few times and quickly figured out that it wasn't just the food he craved. He had a huge crush on a girl he met there and he just couldn't stay away. Actually, they eventually ended up getting married.

According to our estimates, we would each need about $200 for our coast-to-coast adventure. We obviously didn't have that kind of money, so we had to come up with some creative ways to earn it. Somehow we came across quite a few hot automobile seat covers that we picked up for a good price, way below wholesale. Our business plan was to sell the seat covers and then have someone install them for a nominal fee which would allow us to make a good profit. A natural salesperson, Barney made most of the sales. Old Barney could sell ice to an Eskimo.

Barney was a real pro at selling and making deals. For example, he helped me get rid of the 1936 Ford that I had purchased for $50. I had driven the car for a few months without any mechanical problems until we made a fateful trip to Maine. Boys being boys, we pushed that old car to over eighty miles an hour for the whole trip. The radiator overheated and the engine started making strange noises until it totally ceased up. We discovered that the car was not worth the cost of towing and repairs, and I got the brainy idea to sell it "as is" to the highest bidder.

The car had broken down right on the main street of town. We took advantage of the great location and put it up for sale right there. Barney took charge of the situation and sold the car right in the middle of the street, as if he was conducting an auction. In just a half-hour we got an offer on the car. Barney gave the buyer a sales pitch that would make your head spin, including information on the original paint job. He sold the car for $40 and the lucky buyer towed it away with his truck. I was happy to get back most of my $50 investment and was very glad that we would have the benefit of Barney's hustling expertise on our trip to California.

Not long after that, we acquired a supply of "Sable and Pearls", an expensive perfume that we were able to sell at $4 a bottle. Unfortunately, we didn't make much profit on the perfume so we still needed to come up with more money for our cross-country excursion.

We then decided to run a dance similar to some we had attended at

Hanging out with my friends. Left to right: Bobby Agrippino, Barney Lanci, Scott Raggle, Bruno, me, Berrio Gizzi.

the Gardner Ballroom on Massachusetts Avenue in downtown Boston. We hired band leader Tommy Goodman to supply the entertainment. He would bring two bands. The first band, using his name, would play contemporary music. When they took a break, the second band would take over. This band, led by Carmen Valdez, played Latin American music and would be dressed in Latin costume. The evening was a great success, and the guests never realized that the two bands were one and the same. The musicians just made a costume change at the break and played a different style of music. As the promoters of the evening, we were thrilled to have two bands for the price of one.

After all of our efforts, we still didn't have enough money. I was feeling the pressure because everyone else had their share of the expenses except for me. I thought if I could sell my 1939 Plymouth, I could probably get a few hundred dollars for it. I decided to sell it to my pal Cal Bellavia. There was just one problem – he really had no interest in owning a car. I told Cal he would surely need a car sooner or later, and that I had planned to sell my car for $200 but he could have it for only $150. Cal was hesitant, not to mention that he didn't even know how to drive. Using the Barney Lanci selling technique, I offered the services of a mutual friend, Rocky Botta, who could teach him how to drive. Cal was still not interested. At this point, I got so angry that I told him to forget the whole thing. I told him I would not sell him the car under any circumstance, period, and then added that I knew someone else who was very interested in buying the car.

Two days later, I contacted Cal and asked him to take the car off my hands for $125. At this point I admitted that I needed the money badly, and would use it as a stake to get me to California where I planned to fight under an assumed name. I told him I was trying to beat the contract that I had signed in Newark. Cal was furious with me but gave me the $125 for the car. He told me to line up Rocky Botta to give him some tips on driving. I thanked Cal and told him he would not be sorry as I planned to make it big.

I was able to come up with my share very soon after, and we took off for California. We traveled from state to state, gas station to gas station, and restaurant to restaurant. We all took turns at the wheel so we could get to the West Coast as quickly as possible. Once or twice we actually stopped long enough to find comfortable beds and get a good night's sleep. We tried to stretch a dollar as far as we could, especially because we had car problems that we didn't plan for in our budget. Although we were young, we were not gullible, and were frustrated that the local mechanics overcharged us for the repairs. There wasn't much we could do about it though. The repairs had to be done so we could continue on. Of the two Oldsmobiles in our convoy, Barney's 1948 and Jerry's 1951, the '48 gave us the most problems and caused our funds to dwindle. As a result, we had to drive more and eat less.

When we got to Dallas, Texas we decided to check it out. It was a beautiful, clean, and exciting city. We couldn't stay long as the budget didn't allow for any extended stays unless we wanted to consider no meals at all. We were able to find a cheap room in Dallas and proceeded to "liberate" cigarettes from gas stations and hustle food. The cafeteria-style restaurants that used meal tickets to determine the food tab worked the best for us. Patrons would go through the cafeteria line and select their meal…salad, main dish, and dessert. The server behind the counter would punch a hole on the ticket where the price of each type of food was indicated. After enjoying the meal, patrons would present the ticket to the cashier and pay the total shown on the ticket.

We quickly figured out how to work this system to our advantage. We would take two tickets as we entered, putting all of the food on one ticket and the coffee on the other. After we ate our meal, when it was time to pay, we handed the cashier only the ticket for the coffee. The other ticket always conveniently disappeared. Although we knew that this was lousy thing to do, we justified our actions by saying that it was only "small stuff" like cigarettes and food, which we considered to be necessities. Looking back, we probably could have written home and asked our families to send money but, at the time that was not an option we considered. Our finances went from bad to worse and we ended up in a pawn shop making a deal for our rings and watches. The plan was to send for our jewelry once we had some money. No one at home would be the wiser.

Before continuing on to California, we decided that since we were so close to Mexico, we would cross the border and check out the town of Juarez. What we found was a dirty city with filthy streets and dilapidated buildings, certainly not the exciting foreign destination we had envisioned. The few bars we checked out were disappointing too. They were pretty tacky and seemed to be places for the local prostitutes to work out of. After taking in the sights, we decided to cut short our foray into Mexico and get back on the road.

It was a foggy, drizzly night in mid-January 1953 when we finally arrived in Los Angeles. It was disappointing to find cool, damp weather as we had anticipated a hot, dry, tropical climate. We immediately got down to the business of finding a place to stay. Our first stop was the YMCA where we talked with the manager, telling him of our plans, and that I would be boxing once we got settled in the city. The manager sympathized with our financial situation and rented us rooms for "short" money until we found jobs. Once we got settled, Irving went off to stay with his relatives, as planned.

After enjoying our first comfortable night's sleep in quite some time, we explored Los Angeles…uptown, downtown, and everywhere in between. The night life was action-packed with lots of clubs and dance halls. We danced, drank, met and dated some beautiful girls, and partied nonstop. After a few days of fun, we depleted our remaining funds and had to get serious about looking for work. It wasn't as easy as we thought it would be. We drove and walked around looking for work for days without any success. I even went to a construction site hoping to be hired on as a laborer, but again had no luck. My sights were still set on continuing my boxing career once I had the funds to eat properly and the time to adhere to a vigorous training schedule. Of course this also meant I would have to stop my new rotten habit of smoking.

Just like Texas, we survived by beating the tab in the cafeterias or by filling our stomachs with candy bars. Jerry, Barney, and Berrio finally found jobs with the Arrowhead & Brass Plumbing Company, owned by Lou Enterante. After a few days on the job Jerry spoke to Lou about hiring me, and I was grateful to be working very next day. My assignment was to pile up old radiators and mash them in a crusher. I loved my new job because I could take out all my frustrations on those old radiators. After I finished all the crushing, I would deliver plumbing fixtures in the local area. I loved this part of the job too, as I was able to learn the layout of Los Angeles and its suburbs. By this time, the boys and I were getting along rather well. We all had jobs. That meant we were able to eat, party, maintain our cars, pay a little toward our YMCA bill, and even have some money left over for cigarettes. We were having a ball.

We were drawn to the rich and famous Hollywood section of Los Angeles. With its modern architecture and wide boulevards, this section of the city was as different as you could get from Boston. We were drawn to Grauman's Chinese Theatre on Hollywood Boulevard because we never knew which famous personalities we might see there. Our favorite part of the Hollywood scene was, of course, checking out the many nightclubs in that area. We were living it up, feeling like "high rollers" even though we were barely getting buy.

One of the more popular spots at that time was the Hollywood Palladium, a ballroom that featured the famous big bands of the day. We heard it was frequented by famous celebrities so we decided to check it out. What we found was a ticket booth in front of the Palladium with a ticket collector just inside the entrance. The entrance fee definitely did not fit our budget, so we decided to use an age-old plan that we had seen in one of the Dead End Kids movies. Barney was the first guy to approach the ticket collector. He gestured with his thumb that the guy behind him had the tickets. I followed, doing the same thing. Jerry and Berrio were right behind me. As each of us entered the ballroom, we planned to grab a girl and start dancing. Berrio ended up getting stopped by the ticket collector and Jerry turned back to help him out. Jerry explained that we were just getting started in Los Angeles after a long, arduous trip from the East Coast, and that we wanted to be a part of the Hollywood scene.

The Palladian ticket collector, Eddie Forkush, seemed interested in what Jerry had to say. We later discovered that he had a good singing voice and hoped to follow his dream of becoming a professional entertainer. Jerry also mentioned that I was a professional boxer who planned to continue my career in the Los Angeles area. As it turned out, Eddie was a big fight fan and loved the whole story, so he let Jerry and Berrio in. They found Barney right away, but hunted for me all over the dance hall. The guys finally found me in the middle of the dance floor doing a very good job of being inconspicuous. They introduced me to Eddie Forkush and I proceeded to elaborate and exaggerate my goal to quickly get into fighting main events. I even told him that I was ready to fight Art Aragon, who was considered one of the finest boxers on the West Coast. Although he was born in New Mexico, Aragon lived in California. Nicknamed "Golden Boy," Aragon was pegged as a future champion.

Well, the contact was made and we began frequenting the Palladium Ballroom. The price was right. Eddie let us in every night, free of charge. Some of the entertainers who played the ballroom were Harry James, Woody Herman, Les Brown, Hoagy Carmichael and Stan Kenton, just to name a few. They usually booked bands for one or two weeks at a time which was fine with us. We used the Palladuim as our home base, our hangout, and branched out from there to explore everything else that Hollywood had to offer.

In February, we began to look for an apartment. Eddie found us a place just around the corner from where he lived, on Tamourine Avenue, which was conveniently close to the Palladium. There was just one problem, our usual one: money. We had to come up with the first and last month's rent, but we still owed a big balance on our YMCA rent. We would need to pay that up in full if we moved out. As usual, we came up with a plan. First, we needed to get a rope that was long enough to reach from our third floor room at the YMCA all the way to the street. Once we had the rope, we set our plan in motion. We waited until late at night when there was only a skeleton crew on duty to watch the YMCA lobby. There wouldn't be many of the other tenants around either, because most everyone turned in early so they could get up for work in the morning. Shortly after midnight we tied our suitcases to one end of the rope, gently lowered all of our belongings to the street below, and casually walked out of the building. After we were safely out of range of the night crew, we threw the suitcases in the cars and took off for our new apartment. I have to admit it, we were not proud of having stiffed the YMCA after they had been so good to us.

Hollywood was a place to see and be seen, with modern looking buildings, palm trees and movie studios. The hub of the movie capital was the corner of Hollywood Boulevard and Vine Street. There was glamour everywhere with aspiring actors parading back and forth hoping to be discovered by a movie studio executive. We didn't have much time to enjoy the sites during the day because we had to work, but at night the Palladium was ours. One evening I met actor Jeff Chandler there and we hit it off so well that we chatted the evening away. After I told him about my involvement in boxing, he was eager to talk with me. Chandler had recently starred in a fight film entitled, "The Iron Man" and had been required to go through real conditioning to play the role. His training included daily runs and sparring bouts with boxers so he could learn the finer points of ring battle. His goal was to think as a fighter so he could live the part, not just act it.

Our time at the Palladium paid off with introductions to Sammy Davis Jr., and Peter Lawford. Sammy had been a member of the Will Mastin Trio that included his father, Sammy Davis Sr. As a kid, Sammy was the featured song and dance man for the group but he was now trying to make it on his own. Peter Lawford was a British actor who was playing supporting roles in Hollywood at the time. He later married Patricia Kennedy, and became our future president's brother-in-law. Long after our time in California, the famous Rat Pack including Frank Sinatra, Dean

Martin, Joey Bishop, Sammy Davis Jr., and Peter Lawford drew standing room only crowds when they performed at the Sands Hotel in Las Vegas. Their films, "Ocean's Eleven" and "Robin and the Seven Hoods," were huge box office hits.

On a couple of occasions, Jerry and I went to the casinos in Gardner, California, where poker was legal and games were on all the time. It was fun while we were winning, but it didn't take long for our winnings to disappear. I quickly learned an important lesson – quit while ahead, or wind up absolutely broke.

Weeks passed, filled with some interesting adventures. Looking back, those adventures while exciting at the time, were good learning experiences. After living and working in California for only four months, we decided it was time to go home while we were still friends. One problem just seemed to lead to the next, and consequently, one conflict to the next. Jerry decided to sell his 1951 Oldsmobile because we had such problems with it on the way out. As soon as it sold, we hit the road.

We still had an appetite for adventure though, so we decided to head home by way of Las Vegas. It was the most exciting city I had ever experienced. We gambled for a few days, trying our luck at the crap tables and with the roulette wheel. When Danny Thomas strolled by, I did my best to make conversation long enough to ask for his autograph. I also met the actor, Eddie Bracken, before we headed out for the open road. I was so enthralled with Las Vegas that I made up my mind to go back as soon as I could afford it.

Because we were all jammed into one car, we were very uncomfortable on the long trip home. It was a relief when we finally made it back to familiar surroundings, and we couldn't wait to share stories of our adventures with our families and friends. Years later I still think about things that we should have done differently during that trip, like beating restaurant tabs and skipping out on the YMCA, but that is how we learn – from our mistakes.

Serving Rip some of Mom's meatballs.

Round 5

Back in Beantown

A few weeks after I got back to Boston, my father suffered a heart attack. He was rushed to the Intensive Care Unit of the nearby Massachusetts General Hospital and stayed there recuperating for many days. I realized that I now had the responsibility of financially contributing to my family on a regular basis. One day during this time, I was playing a pinball machine at the New Garden Gym when fight promoter Rip Valenti spotted me and came over. He looked me over and said, "What's going on? You look like you've been hit with all the problems in the world!" I thanked Rip for his concern and explained that I was just back from California where I had hoped to fight under an assumed name, but that in my four months there, I didn't get to fight at all under any name. I added that I was now back in Boston, out of work, not boxing, and that my father was scheduled to be released from the hospital but there was no money to pay his hospital bills.

Rip expressed his concern and asked why I was not fighting. I told him about the contract situation with Willie Gilzenberg, adding that I had won every match in New Jersey but had received very little money and no recognition.

Rip reassured me that I was a good fighter who just needed a break. He offered to take care of the New Jersey contract for me, and reminded me that I was well-liked in the Boston area. He then told me that Phil Buccola was impressed with me. That gave me a thrill as Phil was well known in both European and American boxing circles. Rip was as good as his word, and bailed me out by paying off the guys from New Jersey.

It felt like the weight of the world had been lifted off my shoulders.

Battling with Paddy DeMarco.

Rip Valenti took over as my unofficial manager, and for once I really felt like my career was on the right track. I got back into the gym and trained as hard as possible. My "comeback" fight took place on June 13, 1953 against Ken Parsley, a tough cookie. I knocked him out in the sixth round.

Over the next six months, I fought on a regular basis and reeled off another seven consecutive victories, with the highlight being a ten-round decision over the legendary Paddy DeMarco who had fought some of the greatest boxers in the world. My fight with Paddy was brutal, but it was a launching pad that got me to the next great level of competition in the boxing world.

I was really beginning to make a name for myself nationally. The next year, 1954, would be my major step to the crown.

Celebrating victory after the Paddy Demarco fight. Left to right: Frankie Campbell, Bobby Agrippino, Al Clementi, Sammy Fuller, and me.

Help From Above

My religious beliefs have always been private and I rarely speak about them to anyone. In my opinion, discussions about religion or politics just lead to confrontation. People with differing points of view are not right or wrong. They are just different, and I respect this. Having been exposed to people who argue which religion is the right one has taught me to keep my beliefs and practices to myself.

Wilbur Wilson was a very good boxer and a main event fighter in the Boston area. His winning strategy was a constant barrage of punches to wear down his adversaries until he finally knocked them out. I met Wilson at the New Garden Gym when he was a full-fledged welterweight at 147 pounds. I was still fighting as a lightweight at 135 pounds, but we sparred and worked out together every day for a few years. At this time, he was a bit more accomplished than I, but as time passed, my skills improved until I was ready for any opponent.

In fight circles, you never know who your next opponent will be. Wilbur Wilson turned out to be my next opponent. It was now time to see who was better in the ring, and besides, it would be a nice payday for both of us. The match was acceptable to me, as I felt ready for a tough fighter like Wilson. After reflecting on all of the training that we did together, I felt like I could expose his weaknesses, and knock him out. Sportswriters from the local papers didn't quite see it that way. They did not think that it was possible for me to KO Wilson.

As the fight approached, I was considered the underdog. Standing in my corner, I stared at my former sparring partner, met him in the middle for the fight introductions, shook his hand, and waited for the bell. For ten rounds, we battled back and forth, both landing hard shots to each other. I caught him with many combinations of lefts and rights. He continued to absorb everything I had without relenting. I won the fight that night by a decision but, in retrospect, they didn't come any tougher than Wilbur Wilson. I was proud to have fought such a tough warrior.

Everyone felt that Wilson deserved a return match. It didn't take long for our managers to meet and put together a deal for a second engagement. Actually, it was set in stone on the day after our initial fight. This time the money would be much better, and I was happy to partake in war for the $3,000 purse.

I got serious about my training and was back to my old routine of running in the morning at Jamaica Pond, and working out at the New Garden Gym on Friend Street in Boston. My sparring partners were boxers in training for their respective fights and they really kept me in shape.

As luck would have it, I injured my left hand while sparring with a couple of good fighters like Tommy Nee of South Boston, and Johnny "Pie" Arrigo from my North End neighborhood. I foolishly kept the injury to myself, treating my hand with ice, in hopes the soreness would subside quickly.

I didn't have much time for my hand to heal as my rematch with Wilson was coming up very soon. I had predicted a knockout win for our first fight, but knew that I couldn't make the same prediction for the upcoming match considering my injured hand. Also, Wilson had absorbed every punch I threw at him during our first bout and kept coming back

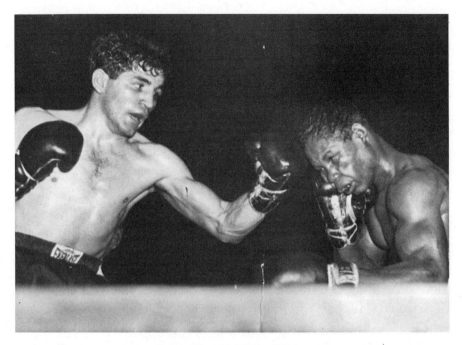

Connecting with Wilbur Wilson.

for more. I began to worry about the outcome of our upcoming event.

Things were not going well, and I turned to my Catholic upbringing thinking that it would help me get through this fight. I thought that if I spoke to God, he would help me in my time of need. I went to church on the day of the fight. Actually, I did this on the morning of every fight, in search of spiritual guidance to gain victory. When I fought on my home turf, I headed for St. Mary's Church in the North End. That day, when I got to St. Mary's, a special Novena was in progress. The pastor of the church noticed me while he was celebrating the service. He approached me from the altar, placed a religious relic in my left hand, and wished me luck. Suddenly, I felt a surge of strength in my left hand and a feeling of great assurance come over me.

That evening, as I entered the ring and shook Wilbur Wilson's hand, I had more confidence than ever before. At the sound of the bell, I came out with a flurry. I blistered him with combinations, and at the end of the round, felt that something special was going to happen. When the bell rang for the second, I felt the same type of surge I had experienced in church that day when I held the relic in my hand. I hit Wilson with a punch no harder than any I threw during our first meeting but, this time, he hit the canvas and was counted out. I had hit Wilson with my injured hand, connecting with a left hook and it was all over.

I felt no pain at all, and could only attribute my immediate recovery to God's handy work. That night, I got help from above.

I was now fighting some of the best fighters in the country and continued my winning streak. Carlos Chavez and Johnny Cesario were my next two opponents. I beat them both. My record now stood at 42-5.

Training for my First Fight at Fenway

Gene Kowalski was the best bartender in town and a great guy. He and I were pals in the early 1950s. Gene was a real joker and I could always count on him to cheer me up if I was down. When I was a bit younger, Gene would lend me his 1936 Plymouth whenever I had a date. If he happened to have a date on the same night, we would double. He was a pal.

In June of 1954, I started training for a match with the great George Araujo. This would be my toughest opponent yet. It was to be held at Fenway Park, the home of the Boston Red Sox. I was now a very established fighter and was thrilled to be fighting at Fenway. I trained in an unusual place located in Acton, Massachusetts, a small town west of Boston. Former wrestler "Dropkick" Murphy had a retreat for recovering alcoholics with beautiful grounds surrounding it. The facilities were perfect for my training and since I would be living there, I didn't need my car. I decided to let my pal Gene use the brand new 1954 Chevy Belaire that I had just bought.

My training was going well. I felt sharp both mentally and physically. One morning after a long run, I sat down to breakfast and picked up a Boston newspaper only to read that I had been involved in a brawl a few miles north of Boston, at Revere Beach. Of course that was not the case because I was training in Acton. I had to get to the bottom of this and try to repair the damage to my reputation. I suspected that Gene had something to do with this.

Apparently, Gene had been hanging out at Revere Beach while I was training in Acton. One evening, four punks looking for trouble started to pick on Gene and two of his pals, Joe Volpe and Junior Troisi. What the troublemakers didn't expect was that Gene, Joe and Junior were street brawlers. They proceeded to flatten the four guys. Gene and his pals had used my car to get to the beach, so that's why my license plate number was taken and reported to the police. Of course, the plate was traced to one Leonardo Liotta of Fleet Street in Boston's North End, and that's why it was reported that I was involved in the brawl.

When the police came to our house, one of my sisters told them that the car was mine but that I was out of town training for an upcoming fight. Gene and the guys then told the police the entire story before it got blown out of proportion but, unfortunately, the damage was already done. Gene returned the car to me at Dropkick Murphy's place in Acton but I was pretty ticked off at him. Because of this incident, we didn't speak for many years.

Good friendships, however, are hard to come by. As time went on, Gene and I eventually buried the hatchet, and resumed our great relationship. He was a good man. I still see Junior Troisi at the Sons of Italy Social Club. Joe Volpe moved to Las Vegas and joined me when I boxed in exhibition matches. Still a tough street fighter, Joe took on many opponents including greats like Mike DeJohn and Jake LaMotta.

Even though the situation with Gene distracted me for a time, I continued on with my training. I was in fantastic condition and more than ready for the match with Araujo on July 12, 1954 that was getting national attention. I came out throwing combination punches to the head and body. George was a tough fighter, but that night I would not be denied. The fight ended in the fifth round on a technical knockout. All of a sudden I, Nardo, aka Tony DeMarco, was becoming known throughout the country. My dream was finally becoming a reality.

The Christmas Show

Bobby Agrippino contacted me about participating in an All-Star Boxing Show and wanted to make sure that I could commit to a date in December of 1954. Once things were set in motion, it was determined that I would be the top bill of the evening with a guaranteed purse of $5,000. I was making a name for myself across the country, and sure could use the money to help my family. My opponent was to be Joe Miceli, another fighter known for his lethal left hook. Joe was a rated contender from New York and he was definitely someone to worry about. Bobby told me that I had been made a 2-1 favorite. Then he added, "I think you can knock him out." My answer was, "I'm not concerned with the odds. My only concern is winning the fight, period." Workouts started the following Monday.

The sports broadcasters and writers announced the event the following day. The undercard was to consist of three other ten-round matches, one six-rounder, and one scheduled for four rounds. The other main event fighters on the card were Willie James vs. Ed Sanders and Tommy Collins vs. Lulu Perez, but the top event of the evening would be my ten round match with Miceli.

Monday morning arrived and, as always, my father called to wake me up and start my morning run. Pa preferred going to Jamaica Pond rather than the Charles River for the workout. As a matter of fact, I preferred the jog around Jamaica Pond as it was a comfortable place to run. The distance is a mile and a half around the path, from start to finish. My routine was to run around once and then build myself up to three and four times without stopping. This was in addition to long walks each night around Boston and sparring at the gym with competitive boxers.

It didn't take me long to get my competitive juices flowing again. I'm talking about the emotional high that came from aggressive training and the knowledge that I was in the best possible condition I could be in. That emotional high is a key component in creating the attitude necessary to win. Anyway, the feeling was back and it stayed with me. One of the secrets of training for a fight is to never under or over train. A good trainer knows when to call it a day. If his fighter doesn't realize this he has to be reminded. I conditioned my body for weeks, right down to the last sparring session.

The last round of my last sparring session turned out to be a nightmare. My sparring partner, Tommy Montgomery, was a tough, wild boxer who gave me a great workout. During that last sparring session, he decided to remove his headgear for some reason. The bell rang for the last round, and we shook hands and began sparring. As we traded punches we worked ourselves in close to each other in the center of the ring. Tommy accidentally came up with his head and due to our close proximity, it slammed into my chin from below. The blood began to flow almost immediately and the gym, which was full of reporters, managers, fighters and spectators, went wild. My trainer, Sammy Fuller, jumped into the ring to see how much damage had been done. He found a two inch cut that looked very bad and Rip Valenti called our doctor for an emergency appointment.

There was no getting around it, the fight was called off. I ended up with twenty-five stitches under my chin and there was no way I would be allowed to fight. I was going to have a long healing process ahead of me to deal with.

The All-Star Boxing Show had been billed as a Christmas event. That year I had no desire to wish anyone a Merry Christmas.

In the Ring

The difference a good fight manager can make is amazing. I was beginning to really establish myself as a world class fighter. Every good fighter needs a manager who can both mentor and strategize. The great Rip Valente had been involved in boxing for many years, and I believed that he was that man. Rip was both a teacher and student of the fight game. He knew the strengths and weaknesses of fighters, and was a great strategist. My career soared after Rip Valente became my unofficial "handler." Promoters were not allowed to manage fighters, so Bobby Agrippino was still my legal manager, but Rip really made the decisions from that point on.

With Rip at the helm, I soared through the ranks. Over the last year, I had established myself because I had a great team in place. Rip, Sammy, great sparring partners, along with my hard focused training, all added up to a winning combination.

The guys that I fought were all world class fighters. Paddy DeMarco, Teddy Davis, Carlos Chavez and Johnny Cesario were all contenders. Davis and Cesario fought some of the best, and Paddy DeMarco's fight with the legendary Willie Pep was historic. Paddy was from Brooklyn, and we used to kid about being related. I finally told him that DeMarco was only my professional name, and I didn't think we had any family ties.

In any event all of these men were great warriors. For example, George Araujo compiled a 58-9-1 record over his great career, Johnny Cesario was 86-14-4, and Paddy was 75-26-3. It was such a great feeling to know I had beaten some of the best in the world.

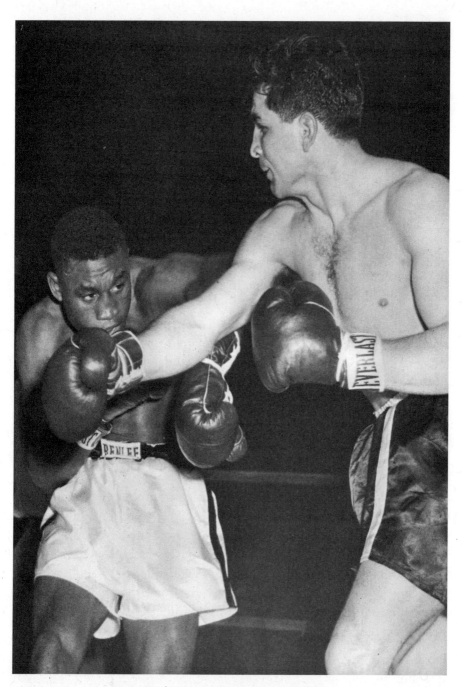

My bout with Jimmy Carter, February 11, 1955.

Going into 1955, I was scheduled to fight the great former Lightweight Champ Jimmy Carter who had compiled an impressive 81-31-13 record over his stellar career. The fight took place in Boston on February 11, 1955. Quite frankly, the fight with Jimmy was not one of my better performances. However, I was sure I had won that contest. I was disappointed with the decision that favored Carter and thought that the judges had misjudged my performance. I accepted the decision, and vowed to get better.

I had to establish myself as a welterweight rather than a junior welterweight in order to fight for a championship, because there was no junior class crown. This meant I had to gain some weight to move from my 140 pounds to at least 147 pounds to qualify. At 140 pounds, I was too small to be welterweight and to big to be a lightweight.

At that point in my career, I was finally earning good money with each fight as the purses were no longer small. I was making three, four, and five thousand dollars a fight. Back in the 1950s, this was a great payday. Things got even better when television began broadcasting boxing. When I fought Paddy DeMarco, we each received $2,500 for the television rights in addition to a percentage of the gate.

One of the sponsors, Phillies Cigar Company, had an arrangement to black out the fight inside a 100-mile radius of Boston. We hoped that this would entice more people to buy tickets to see the fight in person at the Boston Arena rather than watch it on television. If this were to happen, there would be more money coming in at the door which, of course, would increase the size of the purse for each fighter.

The Gillette Company put together a Friday evening television spectacular for boxing fans. It was called the "Gillette Cavalcade of Sports," and the agreement was to pay the boxing promoters more than any other sponsor could. This gave the fighters roughly $4,000 for appearing on television, plus a percentage of the gate. Gillette did make one stipulation; there would not be any broadcast blackouts for the immediate area where the fights were to take place. This would allow fight fans to watch the Friday night matches from home or the local bars. To the fighters, it looked like Gillette would receive the lion's share and we would receive the same amount of money no matter how the broadcast was handled.

The Phillies Cigar Company events had the bigger gate due to the local blackout concept. If the fight was a championship, however, everything was handled differently. When a sponsor backed a championship fight, there would be substantially more money involved. The difference in the purse was determined by the popularity of the boxers, with some receiving as much as $100,000 per fight for participation in a championship bout. I thought things looked great for my future as a boxer. If all worked out as planned, I could quit my day job as a construction worker and concentrate on training. That way the entire fight game could actually become easier and better.

Boxing is as difficult to break into as most professional sports. Getting your foot in the door is the hardest part. When you are just starting out, the system seems to stonewall you. Once you do get your foot in the door and prove yourself, opportunities arise that you didn't even realize existed. For many of us, this meant a lead-in to main events.

I literally took my lumps for five years before making the grade financially. It was time to take the next step up the ladder of success. I relied on Rip Valenti to steer my career in the right direction. Rip seemed to know people from every walk of life: doctors, lawyers, politicians, business people and just about everyone in the fight business. He knew how to cultivate these associations with poise, honesty and finesse. Rip had a style that was warming to people, whether it was in a social or business setting. One of these people was a newspaper pressman named Louie Badaracco. Louie worked at the *Boston Record American*, the city's evening tabloid. Rip and Louie both came from the same part of the North End. Louie was a big fight fan and got to know many of the boxers. One in particular was a hard hitting featherweight named Tommy Collins. Tommy was very close to Rip, who treated him like a son. He even lived with Rip until he married later in the 1950s.

I got to know Louie through Rip and as time went on, we became close friends. I recall seeing Louie at Rip's Ye Garden Café located on Friend Street across from the New Garden Gym. Louie would sometimes drop by and have a drink with Rip and some of his friends who frequented the Café.

One night a stunning beauty entered the Café. I was amazed to learn she was Louie Badaracco's daughter, Maria. Everyone admired Maria and treated her with respect except for Frank "The Fastman" Valenti who got away with teasing her. Frank was Rip's oldest son and had known Maria since they were little kids. He would tease her by saying, "Daddy, daddy, it's time to leave now." I never thought I would get to know Louie or his daughter Maria. In time, however, I got close to both of them. Years later, after Louie's untimely passing, I became like a younger brother to Maria.

Louie was the kind of guy who liked to treat his friends to dinner at the best restaurants and he always included Tommy Collins and me in the group. Because of Louie and Rip, I became familiar with many popular restaurants. Some of their favorite places were Dinty Moore's, Charles Steak House, Locke-Ober and China Sails. I was also invited to theater and sporting events. The good life was beginning to take root.

Clowning for the camera with my sister Mary.

Round 6

My Dream, My Destiny

I was becoming very well known not only in the city, but in the boxing world, nationally and internationally. One night while dining in one of his favorite restaurants, Rip and I got into a very deep discussion about my accomplishments thus far. I had beaten most of the great fighters in the Welterweight Division and was regarded as one of the hardest punchers in the game. My record of 45-6 at the time included wins over the best in the division. It was now time to climb to the top of the mountain. Rip thought that I was ready to fight for the World Welterweight Championship.

It was time to face the Champ, Johnny Saxton. From the age of 12 when I started boxing at the Boys Club, I fantasized about someday being the World Champion. Never in my wildest dreams did I think that this would all come to fruition. I was now fighting for my mother and father, my family, friends, the people of the North End, and my fans across the country.

It was the defining moment in my life to that point. This was my opportunity to leave a lasting impression. I would not fail. I was determined to win the World Championship.

The title fight with Johnny Saxton was set for April 1, 1955 at the Boston Garden. I couldn't wait to start training. Rip set everything up so I could stay home and work out at the local gym instead of heading for training camp. I felt more comfortable staying in Boston where I could walk to the gym and enjoy the support of friends along the way. I established my own routine that included walking to different parts of Boston every day as part of my training. When I wanted more wide open spaces, I would walk through Boston Common or along the banks of the Charles River.

In training.

I have been to many cities, but have never seen a river view as beautiful and welcoming as the Charles. It was home, and it was simply beautiful.

My regular area for running was around Jamaica Pond, part of Boston's Emerald Necklace. During the 1800s, the city of Boston hired landscape architect Frederick Law Olmsted, the designer of Central Park in New York, to create an interconnected series of parks, walkways and ponds to enhance the beauty of the city and be used by residents for recreation. Olmsted completed the job around the beginning of the twentieth century, and the Emerald Necklace became one of my favorite places to train.

When I ran around the pond, I brought my father with me. He liked to keep time and have a towel ready for me to wipe the perspiration from my face. Because of some health issues, Pa had been forced to retire. Helping me train with these small responsibilities gave him great pleasure and a sense of feeling needed. It allowed him to be part of my professional life. Pa took on the responsibility for making sure I maintained healthy habits, and he did everything in his power to make sure I followed a good training routine.

Prior to the match, I had only seen Saxton fight on television. I knew he was from Newark and a great fighter, but I really did not know much about his style. My trainers spent hours studying his strengths and weaknesses and all of my sparring partners tried to imitate his style. Saxton had beaten Kid Gavilan for the title in October 1954. His record before our fight was 46 wins, 3 losses 2 draws.

I was even more dedicated to my training regimen than ever before, as I was absolutely determined to beat Saxton. Sammy Fuller, one of the best trainers in the country, worked me as hard as possible. He developed extremely grueling sessions designed to sharpen all of my skills. My daily running was greatly increased, and my sparring partners were the toughest that could be found. One of the rough and tumble, fighters brought to Boston to work with me was Irvin Steen, a man who had boxed with the best and sparred with many champions. Some of the other sparring partners that were hired to work with me were the ever tough Tommy Nee, Willie "Pineapple" Stevenson and my first boxing teacher, Frankie Ross.

As the day of the fight neared, the media really zeroed in on the fact that the match would take place in my own neighborhood right at the fabled Boston Garden. Dave Gordon, a reporter for the *Boston Record American* predicted that I would win. Herb Ralby and Tim Horgan, two local sportswriters concurred with Gordon's assessment. Dave Egan printed bold headlines announcing "DEMARCO WILL BE THE NEW WELTERWEIGHT CHAMPION!" The Boston writers were going nuts. They were doing everything possible to support me on my quest for the belt. Unfortunately, the odds coming out of New York gave Saxton a 2-1 edge. Those New York reporters did not realize the ability and determination of the kid from Boston.

Two Gladiators ready for war.

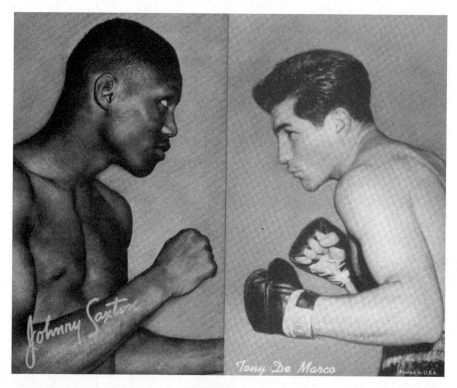

Johnny Saxton

Tony De Marco

Printed In U.S.A.

The Fight

On fight day, I went to the Arch Street Chapel in downtown Boston where I meditated and asked the Good Lord to carry me to victory. With His help, I would not be denied. That night the Boston Garden was jammed. Enthusiastic fans, eager to see one of Boston's own, were almost in a frenzy. They dearly wanted to see me become the undisputed champion. If I could persevere, I would be the only undisputed champion from Boston proper since the great John L. Sullivan. The pressure was unbelievable, but I honestly felt in my heart that I would not be denied.

In the dressing room, it was always important for me to have my close friends with me. These were the people who knew me best, friends like Fernando, Cal, Lindy and Dante. I needed that comfort zone, and my friends provided it. In the dressing room with my friends, after my hands

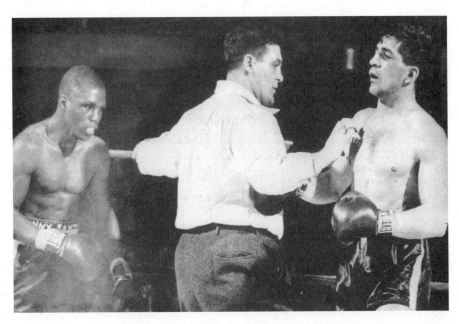

Mel Manning separating Johnny Saxton and me.

were taped, I always had the same routine. I would pump myself up by
shadow boxing while talking aloud. "I am the best. I am the greatest. I will
knock him out. I will hit him with combinations that will put him down."
These affirmations gave me the strength and the determination to win.

My sisters Josephine and Mary were ringside, but our parents never
attended my fights. They always chose to stay home and wait, hoping for
their son to be victorious. The odds remained a strong 2-1 in favor of Saxton, but the odds didn't make any difference to the people in my corner.
They were confident that I would be the new champion. I had gained self-
assurance through meditation and felt confident that I would be the victor.

The crowd noise was at fever pitch as I walked the pathway to the
ring. The closer I got, the more my friends and fans shouted encouragement. I was moved. I climbed the steps and entered my corner of the ring.
As my manager and trainer gave me last minute instructions, they had to
yell over the shouts of the crowd. I looked at the people sitting ringside,
recognizing many of them. All were waving, smiling and screaming words
of encouragement as I sat waiting for the referee to call Saxton and me
to the center of the ring. I told myself that, with God's help, I wouldn't

disappoint the fans. I was ready. This was the moment that I had worked for all of these years. It was almost surrealistic.

After introducing several celebrities in the audience, the ring announcer, Freddie Russo, said in his booming voice, "Ladieees and gentlemen, tonight we have a fifteen round fight for the Welterweight Championship of the World." As is customary, he introduced the challenger first, "Weighing in at 145 ½ pounds, from Boston, Massachusetts, the challenger with a record of forty-five wins and six defeats, the Flame and Fury of Fleet Street, Tony Demarco!" The cheering was deafening and seemed never to end. When Saxton, the reigning champion was introduced, the cheering for me had not yet subsided.

Mel Manning, the referee, gave the instructions to each of us before we went back to our corners to wait for the bell. We stared at each other from our respective corners. It seemed as though our eye contact brought us closer and closer to the middle of the ring. We were both eager for the fight to start. The bell finally rang and we charged on one another, hurling leather. This was the defining moment.

Immediately I threw punches to Saxton's head and body. I seemed to get the best of him with my body punches. The fact is that body punches don't knock you out but they have a devastating effect on your stamina. It was certainly the case with this fight. Between rounds my trainer, Sammy Fuller, told me to keep using body punches and not to let up. I continued to throw body punches at every opportunity. We went back and forth, round after round, but the body shots on Saxton were finally taking their toll. Whenever I could, I threw left hooks and continued until I could see that they were hurting Saxton. Johnny was a devastating puncher, and believe me, he was inflicting some real punishment on me, but I began to wear him down

The excitement mounted with every round. It got to a point where Saxton and I walked to the center of the ring and just stared each other down until the bell rang to start the round. My adrenaline was off the charts, and I was throwing shots that were coming from left field. A couple of times, Mel Manning, the referee, had to come between us to make sure we didn't throw any punches before the bell rang.

For the first thirteen rounds, the fight seesawed back and forth between the two of us. At the beginning of the fourteenth round everything

Saxton goes down for the count.

changed. I hit Saxton with a combination of punches ending with a vicious right that sent him to the canvas. He was hurt and the crowd went wild. Saxton struggled to his feet before the count of ten. Looking back at his condition at that point, I think it would have been better for the Champ if he hadn't tried to stand up. He was helpless and defenseless as I attacked with punch after punch.

I caught the Champ with a relentless array of left hooks and right crosses that were devastating. I hit him with a total of twenty-four consecutive punches that were right on the mark. The crowd was amazed at the amount of punishment the Champ was capable of taking. Many in the crowd shouted for the referee to stop the fight before it was too late.

After those twenty-four punches, Johnny Saxton, the champion of the world, was dead on his feet. The Champ was helpless and the referee stopped the fight. I, Tony DeMarco, Leonardo Liotta, had reached the top of the mountain. I was the new undisputed Welterweight Champion of the World.

The ring announcer tried to quiet the screaming crowd with no

Associated Press wire photo and caption... "THE VICTOR. Tony DeMarco of Boston is lifted from the ring by his second Sammy Fuller after winning the World's Welterweight title last night (April 1) from Johnny Saxton of Philadelphia in the 14th round of their scheduled 15-round bout. DeMarco won on a TKO."

Celebrating my victory with Rip and Sammy.

success. His only recourse was to yell over their volume. He brought the microphone closer to his lips and shouted, "One of the few undisputed champions from Boston Proper since the 'Boston Strong Boy' John L. Sullivan won the heavyweight crown on September 7, 1892. Ladies and gentlemen, the new Welterweight Champion of the World, Tony DeMarco!"

The crowd went absolutely crazy. The cheers shook the rafters of the Boston Garden and could be heard a quarter of a mile down the street to Haymarket Square. Here I was in my own neighborhood, with all of my family and friends. This was one of the greatest moments in Boston sports history. My trainer, Sammy Fuller, lifted me up as the new Champion, while Barney's brother Lou Lanci and Lindy both jumped into the ring. At that moment I thought about my parents. They would be proud of me. I was now the Champion of the World. I was escorted to my dressing room where there were at least one hundred people jammed into that small area, with another hundred waiting outside the door.

The press interviewed me for more than an hour and when they were ushered out, it was finally time to celebrate with my waiting friends and fans. It was really difficult at first to absorb what I had just accom-

Associated Press wire photo and caption... "MOTHER EMBRACES CHAMPION.
*Mrs. James Liotta (cq) tearfully embraces her son Tony DeMarco, 23, in their home in
Boston's North End early today (April 2) after Tony gained the world welterweight title
with a 14th round TKO over Johnny Saxton. Mrs. Liotta fainted
with emotion at first sight of Tony. Small bandage over cut above left eye is only
sign of battle.*"

plished. I was the Champ. Italian Americans across this great nation were celebrating. I thought about what I had accomplished, and cried. It was the proudest moment of my life. After I finally had time to shower and get dressed, it was decided that we would all go over to the Ye Garden Café where Frankie "The Fastman" Valenti had set up the function room for a celebration that would continue for hours. Before we went over there I wanted to see Mom and Pa. On the way home the neighborhood was alive with people and families calling out from their windows and banging pots and pans in celebration.

When I arrived at home the living room was filled with neighbors who stopped by to celebrate my victory with Mom and Pa. Their son Nardo had accomplished what very few others were able to do. After we left my parents, we all went over to the Café. Another friend, Peter Limone, volunteered to help out with the crowd at the restaurant. A well-respected and popular local businessman, Peter helped by greeting the people who dropped by to congratulate me on winning the welterweight title. A couple of local singers also came to the Café and offered to entertain during the evening. Charlie Vitale and Danny Wilson, two popular crooners, entertained the crowd all night. The celebration went on for hours.

Celebration

The days following my victory were the most amazing of my life. A motorcade paraded me from Fleet Street in the North End to Boston City Hall where the mayor, John B. Hynes, presented me with a plaque from the city and then hosted a luncheon at Ida's Restaurant in my honor. The affair was attended by several of Boston's politicians and business people, including Arthur Fiedler, the conductor of the Boston Pops Orchestra.

At home, the phone rang continuously with calls coming in from everywhere including one from Angelo Picardi in Italy. He was an old friend who had been studying voice in Rome for several years. Angelo explained that he picked up a local Rome newspaper and read that his old pal, "Chubby," had won the welterweight championship of the world. Angelo was excited about all of the publicity that I was getting in Italy and promised to send me clippings from the major Italian newspapers so I could show them off in the North End.

The neighborhood welcomes me as the new champion.

I was inundated with calls and requests for appearances. Local radio and television stations wanted to interview the new Champ. I also got many calls from New York City, including one from Ed Sullivan. He wanted me to appear on his Sunday evening television show. I agreed, and it was quite an experience. The "Steve Allen Show," which was an early version of the "Tonight Show," also called to ask if I could make an appearance. Unfortunately, prior commitments didn't allow me to take advantage of that offer and most of the others that followed. Later on, I did appear on one on the most popular television shows of the day, "Masquerade Party."

The celebration went on for weeks. A few friends and I flew to New York to check out the nightclub scene and eat in the best restaurants. One afternoon, while at the Copacabana, I recognized a white-haired man standing off in the distance. It was Frankie Carbo, aka Mr. Gray. He was

A family celebration with Mom, Pa, sisters Josephine and Mary, my cousin Josephine and spouses.

a well-known, well-respected figure in the fight game as well as the underworld. I had gotten to know him a few years earlier when I was living in Arlington, New Jersey, and I went over to say hello.

One of the performers at the Copa, Sonny King, also approached Mr. Gray to say hello. Sonny was a singer who had started out as a fighter and wound up in show business. At this particular time in his career, he was partners with the legendary Jimmy Durante. Mr. Gray made the introductions, and invited Sonny to join us at his table. Sonny recognized my name and congratulated me on winning the championship. He told me that he had heard I was a sensational fighter and referred to me as "Champ" during the conversation. That was one of those "feel good" moments.

We talked all afternoon about show business and boxing, dropping the names of people we knew in both circles. A little while later,

Mickey Walker presenting me with the B'nai B'rith award.

a group of musicians began setting up their band equipment on stage to rehearse. Mr. Gray informed Sonny there would be a singer auditioning that afternoon who was the son of a friend, and he needed Sonny's expertise to critique the boy's performance. Sonny readily agreed.

When the band was introduced a young man, about twenty-five years old, stepped onto the stage and began to sing. After the kid sang four or five songs, Mr. Gray leaned toward Sonny and asked him what he thought. Sonny reluctantly told Mr. Gray he thought the kid "didn't have it." Mr. Gray hesitated for a minute and then, with a glare, said, "You know, not everyone is a Perry Como." Sonny got the message. He immediately changed the subject.

***

We left New York on a Sunday in early April and returned to Boston. My older sister Josephine and her husband, Vincent Vitale, were waiting

My new TKO License plates.

at the airport to meet us along with my sister Mary and her husband Tony Scolaro. A few of the "Fleet Street Guys" showed up including Cal Bellavia, a boyhood chum who had started boxing with me at the Nazzaro Center when we were quite young. Cal and I used to pound each other with boxing gloves while Mr. Nazzaro, Sr. watched over us to make sure we were fighting fair. I was the best man for Cal when he married Rosemary Alves, and later on, they chose me to be the godfather to their firstborn son, Francis. Cal and I have remained the best of friends, even to this day.

After welcoming me at the airport, my family and friends wanted to find a place where we could get something to eat and talk about my trip. Fernando suggested to Lindy DeChristoforo, our close friend, that he open Joe Christy's Luncheonette for the occasion. Usually closed on Sundays, Joe Christy's was a small establishment that was the perfect size to fit the group of a couple dozen people who came to greet me at Logan. Lindy's young nephew, George D'Amelio, helped out by setting up the tables for the eggplant and pasta that was served. George later became the owner of 5 North Square, a fashionable North End Italian restaurant.

We sat, ate and talked until the wee hours of the morning. Nick Sullo, a boxer and good friend of mine, surprised me with some exciting news that day. He had asked State Representative, Charles Capraro and State Senator, Mario Umana, to submit a proposal to Governor Christian Herter that would give me a special Massachusetts license plate with the letters "TKO" on the face in honor of my championship victory. Rocky Marciano was the first to receive this type of an honor after he defeated "Jersey" Joe Wolcott and won the heavyweight championship of the world. I thanked Nick for requesting a special plate for me. Vanity and special plates were a rarity in Massachusetts years ago. I proudly displayed my "TKO" plates on both the front and back bumpers of my car. Here it is many years later and I still have that same plate.

***

The B'nai B'rith organization contacted Rip Valente to discuss the possibility of honoring me at their third annual banquet in Boston. Rip agreed. The B'nai B'rith is a Jewish organization that has always been well respected in the Italian community because of their humanitarian and philanthropic endeavors. When they honored someone, they would enlist the aid of actors and sports figures from all over the country to make presentations to the honoree. The year I was chosen, there were several other honorees. Red Sox manager, Mike "Pinky" Higgins, was given an award that was presented by New York Yankees manger, Casey Stengel. Another baseball figure, Joe Cronin, presented an award to Jimmie Foxx, a Hall of Fame Red Sox slugger. Ferny Flaman, the captain of the Boston Bruins, received his award from Milt Schmidt, another hockey great. An award was presented to Red Auerbach, the coach of the Boston Celtics, and yet another to Russ McLaughlin, the retired Dartmouth College coach. Hollywood celebrities, Sid Caesar and George Gobel were also in attendance.

A citation was presented to Sam Cohen for his outstanding achievements as sports editor of the *Boston Record American*, the city's evening

Ringside with Rocky.

tabloid. Awards were also presented to the four heads of the horseracing tracks that were closest to Boston. The presentations were made to Jane Dooley of Narragansett Park, B.A. Dario of Lincoln Downs, Lou Smith of Rockingham Park and Joe Pappas of Suffolk Downs. When it was my turn, the men presenting the award were all world champion fighters: Mickey Walker, Fritzie Zivic, Barney Ross, Jimmy McLarnin, Lou Brouillard, Peter Latzo, Jack Bitton, and Joe Dundee. I was honored that these eight men were brought in to make the presentation to me.

***

My friends from the North End decided to hold a banquet in my honor. They chose Blinstrub's, the biggest supper club on the East Coast, located on Broadway in South Boston. Stanley Blinstrub was always a gracious host and enjoyed having celebrities in attendance. Rocky Marciano was one of the invited guests and sat next to me. It was an honor to be seated with another Italian American who made us all very proud. The chairman of the banquet was Lindy DeChristoforo, who surprised me with a brand new 1956 Chrysler New Yorker convertible. It had every conceivable custom option including a stereophonic record player. High fidelity and stereo were the state-of-the-art innovations in audio sound and I was one of the first to have this level of technology in a car. The party was a huge success and I swore I would never forget the generosity of my friends...I never have.

WORLD RATINGS

(FOR MONTH ENDING APRIL 21, 1955)

HEAVYWEIGHTS
(Over 175 pounds)

World Champion
ROCKY MARCIANO, Brockton, Mass.
1—NINO VALDES, Cuba
2—DON COCKELL, England
3—BOB BAKER, Pittsburgh, Pa.
4—EZZARD CHARLES, Cincinnati, O.
5—TOMMY JACKSON, Far Rockaway, N. Y.
6—EARL WALLS, Canada
7—REX LAYNE, Lewiston, Utah
8—HEINZ NEUHAUS, Germany
9—JAMES J. PARKER, Toronto, Can.
10—CHARLEY NORKUS, Jersey City, N. J.

MIDDLEWEIGHTS
(Not over 160 pounds)

World Champion
CARL (BOBO) OLSON, Honolulu, T. H.
1—JOEY GIARDELLO, Philadelphia, Pa.
2—CHARLEY HUMEZ, France
3—ROCKY CASTELLANI, Cleveland, O.
4—HOLLY MIMS, Washington, D. C.
5—GUSTAV SCHOLZ, Germany
6—RONNIE DELANEY, Akron, O.
7—EDUARDO LAUSSE, Argentina
8—JOHNNY SULLIVAN, England
9—BOBBY DYKES, Miami, Fla.
10—GIL TURNER, Philadelphia, Pa.

FEATHERWEIGHTS
(Not over 126 pounds)

World Champion
SANDY SADDLER, New York, N. Y.
1—TEDDY DAVIS, Hartford, Conn.
2—PERCY BASSETT, Philadelphia, Pa.
3—RAY FAMECHON, France
4—CIRO MORASEN, Cuba
5—HOGAN (KID) BASSEY, Nigeria
6—RUDY GARCIA, Los Angeles, Calif.
7—CARMELO COSTA, Brooklyn, N. Y.
8—JEAN SNEYERS, Belgium
9—BILLY KELLY, Ireland
10—ORLANDO ECHEVARRIA, Cuba

WELTERWEIGHTS
(Not over 147 pounds)

World Champion
TONY DeMARCO, Boston, Mass.
1—CARMEN BASILIO, Syracuse, N. Y.
2—JOHNNY SAXTON, Brooklyn, N. Y.
3—VINCE MARTINEZ, Paterson, N. J.
4—RAMON FUENTES, Los Angeles, Calif.
5—MAURICE HARPER, Oakland, Calif.
6—HECTOR CONSTANCE, Trinidad, BWI.
7—DEL FLANAGAN, St. Paul, Minn.
8—KID GAVILAN, Cuba
9—CHICO VEJAR, Stamford, Conn.
10—FREDDIE DAWSON, Chicago, Ill.

BANTAMWEIGHTS
(Not over 118 pounds)

World Champion
ROBERT COHEN, France
1—RATON MACIAS, Mexico
2—MARIO D'AGATA, Italy
3—WILLIE TOWEEL, South Africa
4—PIERRE COSSEMYNS, Belgium
5—PETER KEENAN, Scotland
6—CHAMRERN SONGKITRAT, Thailand
7—HILAIRE PRATESI, France
8—BOBBY SINN, Australia
9—ANDRE VALIGNAT, France
10—BILLY PEACOCK, Los Angeles, Calif.

LIGHT HEAVYWEIGHTS
(Not Over 175 pounds)

World Champion
ARCHIE MOORE, San Diego, Calif.
1—HAROLD JOHNSON, Philadelphia, Pa.
2—FLOYD PATTERSON, Brooklyn, N. Y.
3—JOEY MAXIM, Cleveland, O.
4—YOLANDE POMPEY, Trinidad, BWI.
5—WILLI HOEPNER, Germany
6—PAUL ANDREWS, Buffalo, N. Y.
7—BOB SATTERFIELD, Chicago, Ill.
8—BILLY SMITH, Atlantic City, N. J.
9—GERHARD HECHT, Germany
10—EDDIE COTTON, Seattle, Wash.

LIGHTWEIGHTS
(Not over 135 pounds)

World Champion
JAMES CARTER, New York, N. Y.
1—RALPH DUPAS, New Orleans, La.
2—DUILIO LOI, Italy
3—FRANKIE RYFF, New York, N. Y.
4—PADDY DeMARCO, Brooklyn, N. Y.
5—WALLACE (BUD) SMITH, Cincinnati, O.
6—JOHNNY GONSALVES, Oakland, Calif.
7—SERAFIN FERRER, France
8—RICHIE HOWARD, Canada
9—ORLANDO ZULUETA, Cuba
10—JOE LOPES, Sacramento, Calif.

FLYWEIGHTS
(Not over 112 pounds)

World Champion
PASCUAL PEREZ, Argentina
1—DAI DOWER, Wales
2—LEO ESPINOSA, Philippines
3—YOSHIO SHIRAI, Japan
4—NAZZARENO GIANELLI, Italy
5—JAKE TUEI, South Africa
6—HITOSHI MISAKO, Japan
7—TANNY CAMPO, Philippines
8—OSCAR SUAREZ, Cuba
9—DANNY KID, Philippines
10—KEENY TERAN, San Jose, Cal.

TONY De MARCO, Fighter of the Month

TONY De MARCO's knockout of Johnny Saxton to win the world welterweight crown, gained for the New Englander the top honors of the month. By his defeat, Saxton dropped from his high post to Number Two spot, making way for Carmen Basilio who is now matched with De Marco for the title.

Less changes took place in the world ratings during the past month than at any time since last December. In the heavyweight division though Cockell will fight Marciano for the title, Valdes has retained the top post.

Joey Maxim lost top ranking post by his defeat at the hands of Bobo Olson and is now rated third. Harold Johnson and Floyd Patterson have each been upped a peg.

Bob Satterfield has been returned to the light heavyweight rankings by virtue of his win over Marty Marshall. He is rated seventh.

Marshall has been ousted and Billy Smith has dropped from seventh to eighth due to inactivity.

Pierre Langlois, badly beaten by Humez and inactive since, has temporarily been eliminated from the ratings to make room for Gil Turner who has won five in a row, his most recent victories being over Joe Miceli and Gene Fullmer.

Bobby Dykes, on a winning streak, is now ranked ninth and Eduardo Lausse of Argentina has been returned to the fold in seventh place. Johnny Sullivan has been upped from tenth to eighth.

Vince Martinez has been dropped from second to third in the welter class due to inactivity. Freddie Dawson is now tenth. His eye trouble has kept him idle. Virgil Akins, due to his draw with Johnny Brown has been shunted out of the first ten to make room for Chico Vejar who is ninth.

Ralph Dupas, on a winning streak, has been upped to first among the lightweights, taking Duilio Loi's place. Loi is now rated second.

Omsap Naruphai of Thailand won the Oriental lightweight title by beating Bonnie Espinosa.

There are no changes in the feather class but several in the bantam division. Peter Keenan has been upped from sixth to fifth. Hilaire Pratesi of France, kayo winner over Andre Valignat in a bout for the French bantam crown, returns among the elite. He holds down seventh post and Valignat is down to ninth from seventh position. Billy Peacock also dropped a peg to tenth and Fili Nava of Mexico has temporarily been eliminated to make room for Pratesi.

Danny Kid of Manila, loser to bantamweight Little Cesar and to Tanny Campo, has been dropped to ninth place. Hitoshi Misako of Japan is ranked sixth. Campo is seventh and Oscar Suarez of Cuba is eighth.

Keeny Teran of San Jose, Cal. has joined the select circle. He's tenth.

Here are the month's outstanding results:

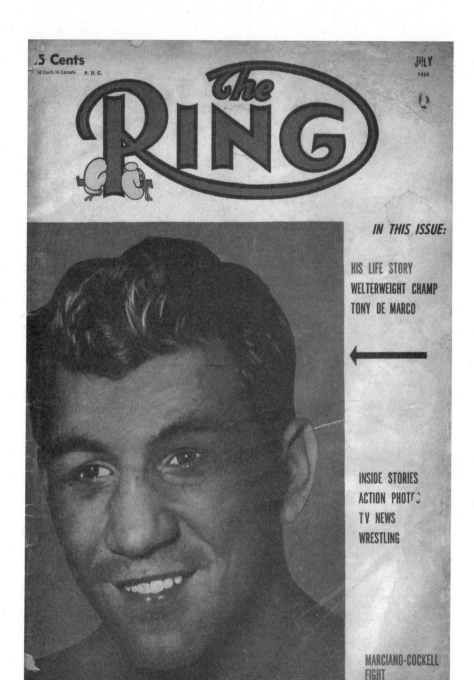

5 Cents
30 Cents in Canada   P. D. C.

JULY
1955

The RING

IN THIS ISSUE:

HIS LIFE STORY
WELTERWEIGHT CHAMP
TONY DE MARCO

←

INSIDE STORIES
ACTION PHOTOS
TV NEWS
WRESTLING

MARCIANO-COCKELL
FIGHT

Round 7

Back To Work

The weeks went by very quickly. After a short vacation in Miami, it was time to start training again. This time I had to defend my championship title. My opponent was to be Carmen Basilio, known as "The Onion Farmer. " Little did I know that this battle would go down in the annals of boxing history as one of the greatest fights of all time, connecting the two of us forever. The Onion Farmer and I would also remain steadfast friends. Since I was the defending champion, and knew that the payday would be good, my team decided we should train in the Catskill Mountains of New York. My manager chose Kutsher's Country Club resort in Monticello, located about twelve mile north of the famous Grossinger's where Rocky Marciano trained before most of his fights. This choice was fine with me.

Rocky committed himself to training as hard as he possibly could. Considered·one of the greatest heavyweights of all time, he and I had a lot in common, from family to food to both being champs from the great state of Massachusetts. Luckily he happened to be in training at that time, so we were able to get together while we were in the Catskills. We dined together quite often and I was proud, like Rocky, to be representing Italian Americans across the country.

Considering that I loved city living, I adjusted pretty well to the country setting of Kutsher's. As I started my training I found that I enjoyed everything about my surroundings. In the beginning, things went very well. I had the support of many friends who visited with the blessing of my manager. My father visited and thoroughly enjoyed helping me with my training. He also loved visiting with the Marcianos, particularly since Rocky's father and Pa had a lot in common. Not only were they both fathers of champions, they were both shoemakers by trade and had many stories to share about coming up the "hard way." In spite of their sons' successes both were very humble men.

Training in the Catskills.

Dinner with Rocky in the Catskills.

Getting ready.

***

The two main components of my training regimen were roadwork and boxing with sparring partners. Basically, the roadwork consisted of running to keep me trim and build up my endurance. Following my sparring rounds, my corner people would critique me and we would make the appropriate adjustments. I was committed to both types of training.

In my spare time, I relaxed in the atmosphere of the country club, socializing with my friends and many of the guests that stayed at Kutsher's. After three weeks, I was really starting to get in the groove with my training when I received bad news from Boston. My good friend, Louie Badaracco, had passed away. Louie had suffered a heart attack during my championship fight with Saxton. He must have been so excited during the fight that his heart gave out. I guess he never fully recovered. From that point on, whenever I thought about my championship win, it was with mixed emotions. It was now connected in my mind with tragedy. Louie was my dear friend, and now he was gone.

Rip made arrangements for me to attend the funeral. I was able to visit briefly with Louie's daughter Maria, who told me how much she appreciated my concern and that she knew how much respect I had for her father. I was torn up inside but there was nothing more I could do. I had to resign myself to the fact that Louie was gone and I had to get on with my training.

The morning after the funeral, Fernando drove me to the airport. Fernando told me that he and Cal were making arrangements to drive to Kutsher's to support me during the last few days before the match with Basilio. This cheered me up as I could look forward to the encouragement they would give me while I finished my training. It was always very important for me to have my close friends nearby to support me before a fight.

I continued to train hard, and felt stronger and in better condition with each day, despite the fact that I was still mourning the death of my good friend. There were, however, a couple of physical issues that distracted me and caused me to worry. The first was a constant nosebleed. The second was a slightly sore right hand that was a result of the shots thrown in the Saxton fight. The nosebleed was nothing new for me. This problem had plagued me during previous training periods.

Jock Semple was now working with me as my masseur. A marathon runner with an exceptional reputation in his heyday, Jock maintained a health spa at the Boston Garden and worked for Walter Brown, the president of the Garden. He was the masseur and physical therapist for the Bruins and the Celtics, but also took care of his personal friends between team assignments. Tommy Collins and I were two of Jock's favorites.

Rip Valenti was friends with Walter Brown and talked him into letting Jock work with me at my training camp. He ran with me every morning and even at the age of fifty-four, Jock had no trouble keeping up with me. Jock recommended that I use hot salt water to treat my nosebleeds. This helped to curb the problem and eased my breathing difficulties. Unfortunately, the salt treatments dried up my nasal tissues and during the fight with Carmen Basilio, I would pay the price.

The Fight of the Decade

One of the reasons Rip picked Kutsher's for my training camp was that we were only about a two-hour drive away from Syracuse, New York, where the match with Basilio was to take place. As fight night approached, Rip decided we should fly to Syracuse the day before the weigh-in. This would give me the opportunity to rest before the fight, and to spend some time with my friends who were there to support me. On the evening before the fight Rip wanted me to try to totally relax. I enjoyed a large porterhouse steak at the hotel restaurant, followed by a card game with my pals in my hotel suite. When the game was over, I watched television before calling it quits for the evening. Watching a few television shows always relaxed me, and I was soon ready for bed. There would be no road work the next day so I would be able to sleep late.

Finally June 10, 1955 arrived. Newspaper reports were plentiful nationally, with predictions coming in from everyone. Boston reporter Tim Horgan wrote that I would retain the championship. Bill Liston wrote a piece on Irvin Steen, my former sparring partner. There were even stories about what I was eating at the training table.

Larry Claflin, another Boston reporter, wrote about a conversation with veteran corner man, Al Lacey, who had worked with some of the greatest fighters in the country. Claflin tried to make something of the fact that Al would not be in my corner on fight night. The truth of the situation was that Lacey had a personal commitment and couldn't be there. Before his departure, Lacey did tell Claflin he believed the fight would go the distance and that I would win.

Austen Lake, a reporter for the *Boston Herald-Traveler*, wrote that he was very surprised I was considered the underdog. John Gillooly, a writer for the *Record-American*, brought up the point that both fighters would be wearing six-ounce gloves which, in our weight class, had been replaced by eight-ounce gloves. Dave Egan predicted that I would win because of my youth, devastating punches, and confidence as the defending champion. Jerry Nason suggested that I might be the hottest underdog of the year in my first title defense. Everyone had an opinion.

This fight was big news in the sporting world and made the headlines during the run up to the match:

DEMARCO'S BOXING IMPROVES	John Akin
APPETITE GOOD, SO CHAMP OK	Tim Horgan
BASILIO 17-10 FAVORITE OVER DEMARCO	Jack Hand
SAMMY FULLER SAYS DEMARCO WILL FLATTEN BASILIO	Bill Liston
DEMARCO FIST WILL WIPE OUT ODDS	Dave Egan
TONY PRONOUNCED FIT	John Gillooly
DEMARCO MUST KO BASILIO TO KEEP CROWN	Austen Lake
FEAR CHAMP BEING RUSHED	Bill Cunningham
VALENTI FEARS LOCAL VERDICT ON CLOSE FIGHT	John Ahern
DEMARCO WILL RETAIN TITLE BUT HE WILL KNOW HE'S BEEN IN A FIGHT	Gerry Hern
DEMARCO'S FIGHT EARLY SELLOUT	Murray Rose
TONY IN PRIME OF YOUTH, READY FOR BOUT. WISHES HE DIDN'T HAVE TO WAIT UNTIL TOMORROW	Tim Horgan
DEMARCO-BASILIO WILL FIND CARMEN NO SAP FROM SYRACUSE	Dan Parker
BOTH SIDES PREDICT KO IN BASILIO-DEMARCO BOUT	Syracuse AP

There were over 12,000 people who didn't care what the reporters had to say. These were the fans in attendance that night at the Syracuse War Memorial Auditorium. Most were there to cheer for Basilio, a native of Canastota, New York, a community near Syracuse. I had my own cheering section of many friends and fans that included Massachusetts Senator Mario Umana, Boston's mayor, John B. Hynes and Francis Bellotti, a future Attorney General in Massachusetts. The judges for the fight were Bert Grant, Frank Foley and millionaire referee Harry Kessler.

In the dressing room, it was all business. "I am the best. I will knock him out. I will not be denied." I was working up a sweat. I was focused. I was ready.

Both Basilio and I entered the ring below the welterweight limit of 147 pounds. As we stepped into the ring for the instructions, we stared at each other. I was going to war with this man. I would do everything in my power to defeat him, and he would do the same. After the instructions from referee Kessler, I went back to my corner, listened to last minute encouragement from my team, and waited for the bell. At the opening, Carmen and I went on the attack right away, throwing haymakers at each other. We were similar fighters, both fearless, hard-punching brawlers. We had both knocked out so many other opponents that each one of us predicted a knockout before the scheduled fifteen rounds would be completed. How does a person judge a fight when both men are gladiators who won't stop throwing punches, and keep staggering each other with devastating blows? I can tell you, it was that kind of a fight.

I was bleeding from my nose right from the first round, but managed to control the fight through the first eight or nine rounds. I was hitting him with some vicious shots and combinations, but The Onion Farmer from New York could sure take the punishment. I took my share of the punishment too, as Carmen was throwing bombs that hit their mark. Quite frankly, both of us took body punches, left hooks to the face and right crosses that would have destroyed most fighters. The first nine rounds were furious. Not until the tenth round did the tides actually change.

We stood toe to toe and peppered each other with shots to the head and body. Dropping my hands for a moment, Basilio floored me with a right, and I hit the canvas. I got up and continued on, fighting to survive the round. Carmen caught me again with a right cross, and I hit the

Battling with Basilio.

canvas again, this time to a count of nine. As I got up, the bell rang ending the round. Coming out for the tenth, I decided to take the fight to him. What the heck, if I was going to go down, it would be with reckless abandon. I went on a relentless attack, but exhaustion was taking its toll. In the eleventh, I went on the offensive again, using every bit of strength I had. Carmen was also exhausted, and to his credit took everything that I was handing out.

Finally, the bloodbath ended late in the twelfth round, when the referee stopped the fight in Basilio's favor. In a great fight on the part of both The Onion Farmer from New York, and the Kid from Boston, I relinquished my crown on a TKO. It was a great battle that could have gone either way. We were both totally drained, but in my heart I thought that the referee should have allowed the fight to continue.

Once I got back to my dressing room, I realized the fight was stopped

Basilio staggered.

because of the way I looked. Actually the cuts were minimal and most were superficial, but they were treated with bandages over my eyes, chin and lips which made me look like I was severely injured.

My buddies and I flew back to Boston, and after receiving well wishes from friends who met us at the airport, I went straight home to Fleet Street. I had lost the championship and was certainly sore after a hard night's work, but most of all I was disappointed to lose the belt. To make matters worse, reporters were coming out of the woodwork.

One reporter even talked himself into my home during the fight so he could interview my parents while the fight was taking place. Mom and Pa were old-fashioned Italians, humble and naïve. They did their best to make what they thought would be the right decision for my benefit, and agreed to be interviewed while watching me fight. The reporter bombarded them with questions at a very vulnerable time. The next day, the headlines read: "Mother Weeps as Heavy Blows Hit Tony; Father Suggests Fight Be Stopped" and "DeMarco's Mother and Father Suggest Fight Be Stopped."

I was so angry that the press took advantage of my parents, that I vowed I would take the necessary precautions to protect them from irresponsible reporters in the future. Most of the reporters were professionals, but there were a few who only cared about scooping the story.

A few days later, I was resting on the first floor of the Fleet Street building where our apartment was located. A car stopped outside and the driver began honking the horn continuously. With my nose still packed in bandages, I looked out the window and saw Mel Massucoo, the picture editor for the *Boston Herald American*, behind the wheel of a flashy convertible. He was a nice guy who was genuinely disappointed that I had lost the championship. Mel had brought along someone to cheer me up with a few laughs. I was amazed to see the great Bob Hope standing in the car and calling for me to come on out and shoot the breeze. I immediately went outside, and suddenly it seemed like the entire neighborhood was there with us. Bob Hope spent a lot of time with us, cracking jokes and hollering to people looking out of their windows. We had a wonderful time with him, and I was very appreciative that he went out of his way to pay me a visit. This was truly a day to remember.

The Rematch

I took a little time off to rest and relax, knowing that before long I would need to begin the process again. This time the fight would be on my turf. I would be in my own element, training at the New Garden Gym. I would be ready.

Rip thought that it would be a good idea for me to have a tune-up fight before my rematch with Basilio. On September 14, 1955, I fought the highly regarded Chico Vejar at the Garden. Chico was a tough kid from Connecticut who won ninety fights over his stellar career.

I had trained like I was fighting for the world championship, and went into the first round with guns blazing. I was fortunate enough to get some very good shots to his head and body, and dispatched Chico in the first round with a TKO. The referee stopped the fight after he hit the canvas twice and was about to hit it for a third time. The fans at the Garden loved it. I was ready for my rematch with The Onion Farmer

The rematch with Basilio was scheduled for November 30, 1955 at

My "tune-up" fight with Chico Vejar.

the Boston Garden. For two and a half months, I trained the same way I had prepared for the Saxton and first Basilio fights. That meant grueling roadwork and fierce sparring sessions with some of the best and toughest boxers around. This time, in my hometown, with my fans and friends to support me, I was sure I would win.

As fight night approached, the media hype intensified. The press referred to the rematch as the fight of the century because of the outstanding battle we had in out first encounter. My team decided I should stay at the Hotel Touraine the night before, and the night of the fight. This would allow me to focus more on the task at hand. The afternoon of the fight, I again went to the Arch Street Chapel to ask the Higher Power to guide me in my battle.

The Boston Garden was packed with a record-breaking crowd of 13,373 fans in attendance that night. The electricity in the building was off the charts. As I walked from the dressing room to the ring, the cheers were deafening. These were my people, and I was going into battle. When the bell rang for the first round, I was confident and ready. Once again, we battled furiously, throwing combinations at each other. I would hit Basilio with a left jab, and he would counter, back and forth, punch after punch. Neither one of us gave an inch.

In the second round, Basilio hit me with a shot that badly split my left eyebrow. As a matter of fact, in that same round, he hit me with another shot that we later learned had broken his hand. I took control for the next five rounds, hitting Basilio with body shots as well as combinations to the head, but he was taking everything that I was dishing out. In the seventh round I staggered Basilio with a left hook that shook his very core. By the eighth round I was in total control, but in the ninth, Basilio staged a great comeback with a brutal body attack on me, that turned the tide in his favor.

The tenth and eleventh were vicious. He was relentless with body shots, which I countered. The body blows took a toll on me, and at that point I was fighting on sheer will. My tank was near empty. In the twelfth round Basilio hit me with a barrage of body punches followed by a vicious right cross, and I went down hitting the canvas. At a count of eight, I got back up, but it was too late. Carmen was on the attack, and hit me with several more shots, concluding with another right, and I went down for good. The fight was over. Carmen had retained the championship.

Two bloody warriors.

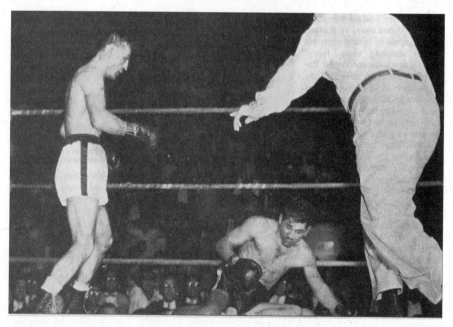

Down I go in the twelfth round.

Little did I know that even though I lost that fight, it would be named the 1955 fight of the year by *The Ring Magazine*, and that the Boxing Hall of Fame would later declare it one of the greatest fights of the twentieth century. I was proud of my two battles with The Onion Farmer and fully realized that I could get into the ring with anyone. I was going to continue on with my career, fight the best, and hopefully make a few bucks. It was time to move forward.

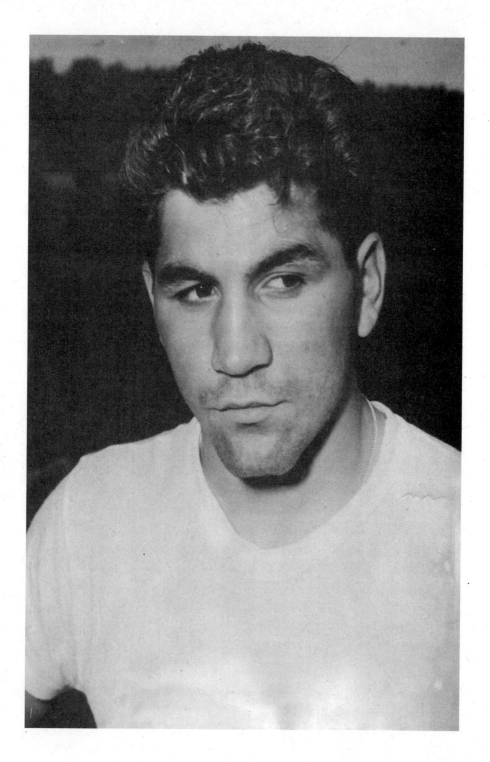

Round 8

Hunting in Maine

My next fight was scheduled for March 5, 1956 against the very tough former lightweight champ, Wallace "Bud" Smith. Rip Valenti decided that I should change up my training regimen to get in condition for Smith. He picked an out-of-the-way place in Maine where I could experience some outdoor conditioning that would include chopping down trees. To make his idea more palatable to this city kid, he promised we would try our hands at hunting while in Maine. This was all to take place before my pre-fight training at the New Garden Gym.

Rip contacted Charlie Miller to help me with this outdoor conditioning. Charlie fashioned himself as one of the world's best outdoor cooks, something I figured had nothing to do with training or hunting, for that matter.

Fernando and I stayed in a small cottage that Rip rented for us. Charlie was bunked more comfortably in a converted train depot near the town of Bemis, Maine. The cottage was worse than any of the cold water flats that existed in the North End. It had no indoor plumbing and only one old-fashioned potbelly stove to heat three rooms. Charlie's place in the train depot, on the other hand, had all the luxuries of penthouse living.

The weather was horrible. It either rained or snowed constantly and because of that, my time in Maine turned out to be nonproductive. There were only a few hours during that period when we could do anything outside, so my time chopping trees or learning to hunt was very limited. The only hunting we had the right gear for was rabbit hunting, which was no fun at all. We would wait around for a half-hour or so at a time in hopes that some rabbits would emerge from the bushes. Most of this time, Fernando and I stood around making faces at each other. The only time we actually shot at a rabbit, we missed. Anyway, with my luck, I'd probably wind up shooting Bugs Bunny, and get every kid in the country ticked off at me.

Charlie Miller decided he would try to get some press for me out of this excursion. He found a pay phone and called Boston sportswriter, Dave Egan, at the *Boston Record American*. The pay phone was outside and it was a bitterly cold day. We could see our breath in the frigid air as we talked on the phone. Charlie told Dave that I was in love with my regimen of running, chopping wood, and hunting in the wilds of Maine. He even went so far as to say that I shot a bear. Fernando was next to me listening to the line that was being handed to the press and all we could do was stare at each other.

As soon as Charlie told Dave Egan that I had killed a bear, he handed me the phone. Egan and I exchanged pleasantries after which, I covered the receiver and growled at Charlie, "Why the Hell did you tell him a story like that?" Charlie whispered, "I promise that you will shoot a bear." He was very convincing, but I didn't understand how Charlie was going to backup his statement. The next day, Charlie told us to walk down the road that led from the cottage to the train depot. He added, "There, you will see a funny looking creature, it's called a bear. We followed his directions and lo and behold, behind the train depot there was a dead bear just lying there. It must have been dead for several days as it was as stiff as a board. Charlie said, "Whether the bear is dead or alive, if you shoot it, you will make my story to Dave Egan legitimate." I really did not like this little ploy, so I just walked away.

Charlie then got a brainstorm. He decided to package the bear and have it delivered to "The Colonel," the nickname everyone used for Dave Egan. The story made the news, but it didn't end up being to my benefit. The so-called giant bear that Charlie had described to the press actually weighed only ninety-five pounds. The story caused an uproar from my fans, many of whom were outraged. Not only was this embarrassing for me, it was against the law in the state of Maine to kill a bear that small. In the eyes of the public I had broken the law, even though I really never shot the bear. Charlie's whole scheme backfired, bringing me publicity all right, but not the positive kind. The entire scenario made me regret the trip to Maine.

Due to the time wasted in Maine, once back in Boston, I had to double my workout routine in order to prepare for the fight with Smith. I must have been very determined because when I climbed in the ring I felt confident and prepared. I guess my determination prevailed. Unfortunately for Smith, he was pretty severely punished. The ref should have stopped the fight sooner. I won the fight in the ninth round by a TKO.

The Battle at Fenway Park

Determined to fight the best in the business, I was scheduled to fight Vince Martinez at Fenway Park on June 16, 1956. Martinez was an excellent fighter with fancy footwork. With twenty-three straight victories, a 48-3 record and devastating punches, Martinez had developed a good reputation, and was pegged as a future champion in the welterweight division. He had his eyes set on the championship, but I had other ideas. I trained as if our meeting was going to be for the welterweight crown.

I worked out at the New Garden Gym in Boston with my sparring partner, Frankie Ross. We had discovered my long time boxer-friend had similar skills as my opponent to be, Vince Martinez. One afternoon, while Frankie and I were sparring, Vince Martinez surprised us by dropping by the gym. I assumed he was there to observe my fighting strategies so I told Frankie that I would throw a punch that would impress the hell out of him. Soon after we began the sparring session I hit Frankie, connecting with a left hook. He staggered and bounced off the ropes. I immediately went to his aid and held him up until he was ready to spar again, and we continued on until the end of the time allotted. I must say that Frankie exaggerated his reaction to my punch a bit. We were just trying to gain a psychological advantage.

People observing the sparring session were quite impressed with my performance, especially the left hook. Among those I impressed was my future opponent, Vince Martinez.

The 15,000 people who attended the fight at Fenway Park really got their money's worth that June evening. I was an underdog going in and, for the first few rounds, Martinez had his way with me. Going into the fifth round, I was behind. As the bell rang, I decided that I was tired of being a clear target for Vince. From the fifth round on, I took the fight directly to him, hitting Martinez with vicious combinations to the head and body. He began to run out of gas by the seventh, and from that point on, it was either a matter of me knocking him out or winning by a decision. Giving credit to Martinez, he withstood my flurry, but I won by a unanimous decision. It was, without a doubt, one of my tougher fights.

I had won three important bouts in a row against tough battlers like former Welterweight Champ Kid Gavilan, Vince Martinez, and Arthur Persley. Then there were the two split decisions that I lost to Gaspar Ortega at Madison Square Garden, a win against Ortega in Boston in 1957, and wins against Larry Bordman and Walter Byars. I was still fighting the best in the world and holding my own.

The Spoiler

My next opponent was Virgil "Honey Bear" Akins, who I will always think of as "The Spoiler." Virgil was a tough fighter who battled some of the best in both the welterweight and middleweight divisions.

My advisors, manager, trainer, and corner man all agreed that Akins would be a suitable and profitable match for me. Even more enticing was the fact that Carmen Basilio had just relinquished the welterweight championship after he won the middleweight championship from Sugar Ray Robinson. Both the Akins and DeMarco camps got together to set things up. We were all of the opinion that the fight should determine the Welterweight Championship of the World.

Unfortunately, the Boxing Commission and fight organizations from different parts of the country, including New York, had other ideas. The New York Commission was opposed, as were some other states. They wanted an elimination tournament to determine who would succeed Basilio as Welterweight Champ.

The New York Boxing Commission added in other ranked and rated fighters. Their list of contenders included Issac Logart, Vince Martinez, Don Jordan and Del Flanagan. Rip Valenti disagreed and decided, along with the Akins camp, and in accordance with the Massachusetts and European Commissions, to go ahead with the championship fight between Akins and me. This "disputed" championship fight was scheduled to take place at the Boston Garden on October 29, 1957 as a fifteen round bout.

DeMarco-Martinez, Fenway Park 1956.

October 29th finally arrived. I had trained, and trained hard. I felt indestructible and climbed into the ring with confidence, the kind of confidence a fighter psychologically needs to persevere against his opponent. Round after round, it appeared that I was winning. I knocked Akins

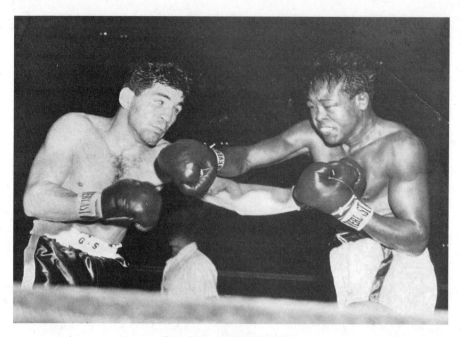

Brawling with Kid Gavilan.

down for the first time in his career. In the middle of the fight, I began slowing down and caught a few punches to the head. Most of the crowd and the people in the other corner just assumed that my apparent fatigue was the result of attacking my opponent with a constant barrage of blows to the body. The people in my corner knew that I had a problem that was never mentioned, especially when the press was around. I had developed hypoglycemia, a blood sugar deficiency, and it began working its strange effect right there in the middle of the championship fight with Akins. I slowly lost my stamina and then, after 14 grueling rounds, lost the fight in a knockout. It was a great crowd-pleasing performance though, which guaranteed a lucrative rematch. At this point in time, the good paydays were important. After all, this was my line of work, and the boxing lifespan of any good fighter is not very long. It was important to make some good money.

Rip immediately made arrangements for me to fight Akins again. Everything was signed, sealed and delivered for a rematch in only two and half months. The fight would take place at the Boston Garden. I recuperated and continued to train but Rip became very concerned about my low

Associated Press wire photo and caption... "NEW YORK, Dec 21...CHIN-UPS... Gaspar Ortega of Mexico, left, takes a right on the chin thrown by Tony DeMarco of Boston in fourth round at Madison Square Garden tonight. Ortega won this 10-round feature by a split decision."

blood sugar and how it negatively affected my energy level and endurance. To help me out, he tried to convince the Boxing Commission to sanction the match as a twelve round championship fight. This was not going to happen and it was scheduled as a fifteen round match.

As usual, I trained to the best of my ability, and on fight night, I stepped into the ring prepared and confident. That was the last thing I remembered. The fight was stopped in the twelfth round on a TKO. I thought that, once again, the hypoglycemia did me in and I was very depressed about what had happened. Here I was, in great shape, training hard, and defeated by a blood disorder rather than my opponent.

This was a scary situation. I felt awkward and uncertain. My emotions hit a legendary low. This was a puzzle I couldn't understand, and the loss of memory during the fight stayed with me. Maybe it was time to re-evaluate my career.

The following day, my friend Cal dropped by and tried his best to

Associated Press wire photo and caption... "BOSTON, JAN.22...END OF THE
ROAD FOR TONY DEMARCO??...Tony DeMarco, one time welterweight title
holder from Boston's north end, examines his battered face in a hotel room here this
morning after taking a bad beating from Virgil Akins of St. Louis, here last night.
Akins won the fight on a TKO in the 12th round of their scheduled 15 round bout.
DeMarco's managers fear it was his last fight."

convince me to leave the defeat behind. He suggested that I might want to consider retirement. The mayor of Boston, John B. Hynes, had offered me a job. After that fight, I started to seriously consider working for him.

I was well-liked throughout local political circles and knew that I would be among friends if I accepted a job working for the city. Not wanting to rush into anything while in such an uncertain state, I decided to wait a few weeks to regroup before making any decisions about my future.

The Mickey

Then the letters started to come. They were sent to a couple of my close friends, Lindy DeChristoforo and Bobby Agrippino. The contents suggested that there had been foul play involved in my fight with Akins. According to the letters, someone spiked the juice I drank right before the fight. I usually drank fresh squeezed orange juice mixed with glucose before I left my dressing room for any of my fights. The orange juice quenched my thirst and the glucose helped to counteract my problems with hypoglycemia.

The letters indicated that the spiking of the juice took place at Bobby Agrippino's apartment while he was visiting his sister in her upstairs apartment. Bobby's visit with his sister was part of his daily routine. They would sip coffee and discuss family business and just gossip. People were always coming in and out of Bobby's apartment. The letters went on to say that whoever spiked the juice mixture, knew Bobby's routine and knew that Bobby was the person who took care of the juice for me. Whatever they spiked the mixture with, I'll never know. On the night of the fight, I drank what I thought was "my usual" and headed for the ring. That is about all I remember. The additive worked so quickly that by the time I reached the ring, I felt like I was operating in slow motion.

The rumors began to fly after I told a few of my closest friends about the loss of memory. When we were all at Lindy's restaurant, Lindy read one of the actual letters out loud. Was it someone in my inner circle or an outsider who was responsible for spiking my orange juice? Even more important, what should be done about it? Bobby wanted to have the letters analyzed to determine if they were all written by the same person. Lindy thought something about the letter seemed familiar. He offered to get writing samples from his restaurant patrons by having them sign their checks, and then have a handwriting expert compare the signatures to the letters. In my mind, the big question was, "Who would do something like this?" We surmised that it was probably one of the guys from the neighborhood, with access to me, who decided to bet on Akins, knowing that he could slow me down with the "Mickey."

The boys didn't want to involve the police, even though it was suggested a few times. We decided to do nothing other than keep our eyes and ears open. I personally was in such a funk that I did nothing for months except play cards in my apartment and think about all of this. Why would someone that I knew do this to me? To this day, I still wonder who did this, and why. It was now 1958, and I was getting tired and disheartened. It was time to take a step back. Maybe I should even retire. In any event, I was going to take a long vacation and ponder the future. I would not fight for over a year.

Outside the Ring

It was a warm May afternoon when my pal Frank "Butchie" Miceli called to ask me to speak at a Civic Association event in Winchester, an affluent suburb of Boston. Butchie mentioned that John Volpe, a big contractor who was a close friend of his parents, would also be speaking at the affair. So, I was to share the bill as main speaker with the man who would become the second Italian American governor of Massachusetts and eventually, Ambassador to Italy. I was getting over my funk and accepted the invitation.

Butchie and I met few years back in Miami Beach when I was vacationing with my cousin, Leo Rossi. He was a great guy with a sense of humor and a lot of personality. Butchie was the type who could create a banquet in the middle of a desert.

After the Winchester event, Mr. Volpe struck up a conversation with Butchie and me. He expressed his admiration for my accomplishments and successful career. As the conversation progressed, Volpe told me that his teenage son, Jackie, wanted to learn the fundamentals of boxing. He asked if I would consider giving Jackie some basic lessons in the art of self-defense, and I decided to meet Jackie and evaluate his interest in boxing.

Jackie Volpe turned out to be a well-behaved youngster who was absolutely thrilled to have the opportunity to learn from the Champ. We soon began workouts and instruction at the New Garden Gym.

When John Volpe later became Governor of Massachusetts, he appointed me to the Boxers' Fund Board. This was an honorary position, but it held great interest for me as one of our goals was to improve the living conditions of boxers.

***

A group of boxers from the Boston area formed a softball team with the sole purpose of playing charity games. The main charity supported by the team was The Jimmy Fund, which was established in 1948 as a collaboration between the Boston Braves baseball team and the Variety Club of New England, with the goal of finding a cure for juvenile cancer of all types. One of the early sports figures to become involved as a spokesperson for the organization was Jimmy Piersall, a famed Red Sox outfielder.

We boxers put a powerful softball team together and won most of our games which were played against the Boston Police Department, the Boston Fire Department, the Boston Parks Department, the Boston School Department and many other fraternal organizations located within the general area. Our main objective was to stimulate donations from people and organizations within the community, but we needed help, so we enlisted the aid of the Maria Stanley Model Agency. Their models possessed the beauty and poise we lacked, and it was a winning combination. They canvassed the crowd as we played ball and clowned around at the ballparks in Boston, and later, throughout Massachusetts. The spectators loved the combination of the beautiful models and our antics on the field. As a result, we did rather well with our fundraising.

As a softball team, we were pretty good. Joe Rindone, a middleweight from the Roxbury section of Boston, was a powerful home run hitter. Another middleweight, Jim Sauer from Cambridge, was a slugger who helped us win. Featherweight contender, Tommy Collins was something else, always clowning around throughout the game. Tommy once showed up wearing green satin shorts, green stockings, a green hat and a green shirt with the inscription on the back reading, "I can lick anybody in the park." Tommy was really the life of the team.

On the parade route with Mayor Hynes and Rocky.

My position was shortstop. It was the same position I played as a kid with the gang on Fleet Street when we played baseball and softball in the old neighborhood. My drawback was hitting. I was not exceptional in this department. However, one time I did manage to "call my shot."

One Sunday afternoon, the team had a game with a fraternal organization in East Boston, at a field called The Boston City Yard. I was scheduled to fight soon after the game and had to take precautions to avoid any strenuous activities or injuries that might hamper my chances in the ring. Basically, I planned to sit the game out, just to be on the safe side. The captain of our team was Freddie Cabral, a middleweight from Cambridge. He asked if I would at least pinch hit just to make an appearance. I couldn't refuse his request and told my date that I was going to be introduced to the crowd and would have to get up at bat just once. I began to brag that I was going to hit a home run and then we could be on our way. I had a cocky attitude and swung at the first pitch. The ball flew out toward center field and continued over the fielder's head. I rounded the bases waving my hat to the crowd. When I returned to the bench, I packed my things and left the park having hit my one and only, ever, home run.

Round 9

Decision Time

I had ten bouts between my last Basilio fight in 1955 and the last Virgil Akins fight in 1958. Between these two points in time, I wasn't sure whether I should cut my career short or hang in there. I was having a few physical problems, including a chronic inner ear infection and a struggle controlling my hypoglycemia. When I was not in good control of my blood sugar level, I would experience an unannounced sudden drop in blood sugar that caused immediate fatigue. My doctor told me I could control the hypoglycemia by strictly following a proper diet, and I tried my best to follow the doctor's orders to the letter.

As the 1960s approached, I realized that my days in the ring were numbered. The up-and-coming young talent in the welterweight division and surrounding divisions impressed me beyond imagination. As I trained, I wondered how I would handle some of these new kids, especially if my hypoglycemia caused my blood sugar to plummet, leaving me exhausted and unable to fight up to the level I expected from myself.

I never discussed my health problems with anyone other than my trainers or my family, not even my best friends. Socially, when the guys and I would get together, we would talk about some of the newcomers to the ring; the boxers, the sluggers, the potential champions, and who their management and training groups were. I kept the discussion away from myself unless it was to answer questions about my future bouts.

Once I was diagnosed with hypoglycemia, my strategy was to maintain the highest sugar level possible when I entered the ring. This was my insurance policy, and it worked for me until I retired. I fought two opponents in the early part of 1959, George Monroe who I stopped in the eighth round with a TKO, and Eddie Connors who I decisioned in ten rounds. After some real soul searching, I decided that it was time to take a little more time off, another year. In the meantime, I was beginning to look for outside opportunities.

Investment Opportunities

One day, I was at Joe Christy's Luncheonette having a cup of coffee when my friend Lindy told me about an investment opportunity that sounded intriguing. A mutual friend, neighborhood insurance broker Carmen Ayelia, had mentioned it to Lindy, and was on his way over to explain it to us. Carmen came into the coffee shop along with John Sterges, a business associate who dealt in oil wells. Sterges had speculated in oil wells in Luling, Texas and he raved about how profitable this venture had been. Actually, he speculated in selling oil wells in Luling, Texas, not in the development of them. In his conversation, he characterized the wells he sold as sure bets and sound business investments.

To make this investment less risky, investors were promised a return of half of their capital if the drilling was unsuccessful. If a well was successful, the other half of the invested money would be used to complete the function of the well. He added that the investment was $5000 for 2/16ths of a 13/16ths share of each oil well. The remaining 3/16ths of the oil well would belong to the workers and dealers. The shares were handled in this manner in order to keep the cost of each share as affordable as possible. Sterges had worked in the oil well business for some time and appeared to be successful. He had realized a good return on his investment with the "Kate Coling I" oil well. The proposal he presented to us was for the "Kate Coling II." Even though it would be a good faith deal, Lindy and I liked the way things sounded. We decided to invest the $5000 for a 2/16 interest in the well.

A month later, we got the best possible news. Not only was the oil well successful, it was considered a "gusher," which meant there was little restriction on how much oil could be taken from the well at one time. This was great news, and we began counting our riches before we received them.

Meanwhile, Sterges attempted to interest some of our other friends in oil well drilling on the same rich land in Luling, Texas. Lindy and I

Chatting with the "Splendid Splinter," Ted Williams.

enthusiastically tried to convince the others to join in on the investment. John Savino, a businessman who loved to speculate on investments, heard about the oil wells. Savino said before he would consider investing the $5000, he would want to fly to Luling to check out the oil wells first hand. John thought it would be a good idea if Lindy and I went along with him, and we agreed.

Travel arrangements were quickly made and, before we knew it, we were on our way to Luling, Texas after a brief overnight stop in Dallas. I had been to Dallas once before during my cross-country trip to California, and had liked the city because it was clean, modern-looking, and had many interesting places to visit. We arrived there in time for dinner and decided to visit a lounge for a few drinks afterward. By chance, we chose a nearby

Here I am with one of my fans, Tony Bennett.

place with a comfortable, relaxing atmosphere that was called the Carousel Lounge. There we met the owner, a middle aged man named Jack Ruby. He was the same Jack Ruby who, a few short years later, shot and killed Lee Harvey Oswald, the assassin of John F. Kennedy.

Ruby started a conversation with Lindy, John and me, and treated us to a drink. I found him to be a pretty interesting guy who seemed to know a lot about health and vitamins. He seemed to be very excited about a new vitamin tonic that was used to heal injured and sick people. Ruby showed us some literature about this healing tonic and spent more than an hour with us. When he had to leave, he wished us success with our oil well.

The next day, we rented a car and headed for San Antonio, an historic city close to Luling. Lindy took the wheel, which was a mistake as he was known for his "lead foot" driving style. This was not a problem on the open road but, when we passed through a small town, we were stopped for speeding. Because of my status as a former boxing champion, I thought

Ringside with Danny Kaye.

it would be best if I spoke with the police officer. Maybe the policeman would be impressed and would go easy on us. In fact, the officer was very excited to meet me. After a brief conversation, the officer said to me, "It's nice to meet you, Champ. I've seen you in action on television and you are very good. You have seen a lot of blood, I'm sure. However, I've seen a lot of blood on these roads. I work with strict rules. So, kindly show me your license and registration." He then approached Lindy and John and went through their papers. The officer then ordered us to follow him directly to what looked like a barn but was actually the local courthouse. There, we saw a fellow who was sweeping the floor. Lindy asked the sweeper where the judge was. The sweeper replied, "I am the judge. I'll be right with you." When he was finally ready, he fined us $50.00 for the speeding violation.

We left the courthouse and drove to the city of San Antonio, home to the Alamo. After enjoying the sights of the city, we finally made it to

Luling and the reason for our trip, the oil well. Kate Coling II was among many other wells in the area. As a matter of fact, the entire landscape was covered with oil wells.

When we were brought to the well, it wasn't at all like we thought it would be. It wasn't under a long derrick as we had imagined from what we had seen in the movies. Surprisingly, it was not the gusher Sterges reported it was. Instead, it was pumping at a trickle. The well was producing next to nothing. At that point we realized we had been swindled. We were angry at Sterges, but were also angry at ourselves for getting into this venture. We vowed to get to get our money back. Any good decisions we made from that point on were due to the guidance given to us by John Savino. If it wasn't for John, we would have probably bought into a deal for a "Kate Coling III."

We went to the Luling town hall to get as much information as we could about the oil wells. Driving back to Dallas for the flight home to Boston gave us a chance to assess the situation and deal with our financial loss. John Savino kept the conversation light and punctuated it with comical remarks to ease the pressure for all of us.

***

The day after we got back from Texas, we called John Sterges to schedule a meeting right away. He tried to put us off, but Lindy didn't give him a chance to refuse. We planned to meet at my apartment, a nice cozy place built by my friend, Fernando, in what had previously been a candy store. Fernando was kind enough to build me a beautiful place with all of the modern conveniences. It was "state of the art" for the time with indirect lighting and a picture window overlooking the patio. Fernando even arranged for a beautiful brick bar to be built by another of my good friends, Primo Iaccobucci.

The meeting with Sterges was to take place on Wednesday of that week at my new apartment, which we called Fernando Place. Wednesday was only a couple of days after we received the disappointing news about the oil well. Everyone arrived on time, so we could get right down to business. Lindy ran the meeting, and spoke for both of us. He began by saying that after seeing the Kate Coling II oil well, we weren't too happy.

The gusher that John Sterges had promised us was nothing more than a dribble. Lindy added that he felt that we had all been swindled.

Sterges replied that he understood our concerns and that he had not intentionally given us false information. He claimed that everything he told us had been based on information that was given to him. Sterges reminded us of his guarantee that if the oil well was not successful, he would return half the money we had invested. Any incurred expenses surrounding the oil or future drilling would not apply to us. Lindy shot back that, from what we saw, there was oil coming from the well, but not enough to generate a profit, and that would mean we would lose our $5000 investment for the 2/16th shares. Sterges made a face and commented that all business investments are gambles.

At this point, I spoke up. I was not happy with the way things were going, and repeated what Sterges told us two weeks before we went to Texas. At that time he told us that the Kate Coling II was a gusher, and when we saw it, it was another story. Sterges explained that when we demanded this meeting, he immediately made a phone call to his associates and was told that there was a problem with the Kate Coling II, and what we observed was the result of it. There was a blockage somewhere in the oil lines which could be repaired, but we would need to invest the money to pay for the repairs. Lindy became angry and told Sterges that there would be no more money, and that it would be in Sterges' best interest to refund our investment. Sterges jumped up and yelled back at Lindy that neither he nor anyone else was going to get any money back.

Lindy became uncontrollable and lunged at Sterges. He couldn't get around the cocktail table to get to his target and, in a rage, he picked up a wine glass by its stem and smashed it in Sterges' face screaming obscenities all the while. There was blood everywhere and he just continued screaming at Sterges. I pulled Lindy out of the way and helped Sterges by getting him a towel for his bleeding face. He rested until the bleeding was under control and then, about half hour later, he told Lindy his money would be returned. He apologetically told me that I would either have to wait for a refund or take part in repairing the well. After Sterges left, I told Lindy that there was no excuse for what he did. I was furious. There is enough violence in the ring. The last thing that I wanted was violence in my home.

Weeks later, after the oil fiasco, I was still looking for some type of business to get involved in. My goal was to build a sound fiscal future for myself. Louie Badaracco's daughter, Maria, suggested that I check out Purcell's, a popular restaurant on School Street near Boston's City Hall. A friend of Maria's was part-owner, and wanted to sell his piece of the restaurant. The original owner, Mr. Purcell, was influential in local politics. In his day, a good many of the city's problems were solved at that restaurant. After his death, Purcell's glory faded and the restaurant became financially strapped. I decided to buy into the business thinking that I could help restore it to its glory days. I didn't need a lot of money to buy in, and I would receive a weekly paycheck. The paycheck was important, because my responsibilities were soon to expand a bit. I had been dating JoAnn Costonis off and on for a few years. As a flight attendant, she traveled a lot, but we saw each other as much as we could. After courting for a lengthy period, we decided to get married. We had a small ceremony with our family and closest friends. Although we planned an outside reception, it rained on our wedding day. As part owner of Purcell's, it was an easy fix to move the reception to the Harvard Room at the restaurant.

After I got married, I continued to work the front door as the greeter five nights per week. In the process, I also promoted the function room for banquets and private functions. The problem was that I still had the boxing fire inside me. After a year, I decided that this was not really what I wanted. I sold my share of the business for more than I paid for it, and was happy to walk away with a small profit. I missed boxing and decided to give it another shot.

The Comeback

I shared my plans for a comeback with Guy Consolo and asked if he would consider working with me as my principal trainer. When he agreed, I told him I also wanted Frankie Campbell to work in my corner again. Frankie started out with me when I was with Coogie and I wanted him back. I told Guy I was not interested in working any longer with Sammy, Bobby or Rip. I wanted to make this comeback on my own. Besides, I

Left to right: Benny DeChristoforo, me, Jimmy Durante, Tony Badarese, Dante DeChristoforo.

hadn't heard from any of them since my last fight which was some time ago. It was time to start fresh again.

Guy agreed to contact Campbell and a corner man like Al Clemente or Al Lacey for a third man. When word got out about my intentions, I quickly received boxing offers. Many looked good. Eddie Quinn, a sharp promoter from Montreal who worked with both wrestlers and boxers was looking for someone to promote in Boston, so he could obtain a Massachusetts promoters license. I had met him earlier in my career when I had a few bouts in Canada after my return from Newark.

In 1960, there were only two boxers in Boston who could be counted on to draw a big crowd, Paul Pender and me. Pender had beaten Sugar Ray Robinson for the middleweight title and was committed to his promoter, John Buckley.

I was the answer for Quinn but, I was not going to be cheap. Quinn approached me but I would not budge until he offered me a piece of the promotion business as well as a 35% cut of the actual fight. The 35% cut and the 25% of the promotion business was guaranteed whether I fought or not. When the contract was drawn up, I decided to discuss it with friends and family even though I thought it looked great. I asked Guy Consolo and Cal Bellavia to help me weigh the pros and cons. They both recommended that I hire an attorney to protect my interests. I retained Bob Caggiano, a lawyer from the North End. Caggiano advised me to find someone to represent my 25% of the promotion. I immediately thought of Dante's brother, Benny DeChristoforo, who was a close friend and someone I trusted implicitly. He was the perfect choice. After a long meeting with Benny and Bob Caggiano, everything was signed and set to go.

A week later, I received a call that I was to fight Denny Moyer, an excellent boxer from Portland, Oregon. The fight was set for February 10, 1960 at the Boston Garden. My corner men told me that I was the favorite. I trained as usual, running in my favorite places, sparring with good opponents and abstaining from cigarette smoking, a habit that was very accepted in those days. When the time came, I was more than ready.

Both Moyer and I came out banging at the bell. We were wild enough to collide, banging our heads together several times. I broke away from the clinch and as I pushed Moyer away, discovered I was bleeding profusely from a cut on my forehead that was a result of the accidental head butt.

I was badly cut, so bad that my forehead was covered with blood and it poured as if it was coming from an open faucet. As we danced around the ring, the canvas soon became stained red. When I was hit with a couple of jabs, blood splattered on a couple of sportswriters and judges sitting in the first row. The referee looked at the laceration on my forehead and said that if I continued bleeding in the next round, he would stop the fight.

As the bell rang for the second round, common sense told me that there was only one way to win considering my physical situation. I'd have to knockout Moyer. A knockout isn't easy against a good fighter and Moyer was that good. It didn't matter – before the second round really developed, the referee stopped the fight. It should have been called a "no contest," but Moyer was called the winner by a TKO. This was a tough break for Eddie Quinn but an even tougher break for "The Flame and Fury." This time I hadn't lived up to the nickname. The "Flame" went out pretty quickly, albeit by a fluke head butt.

Payoff time came the next day and my cut was 35%, which netted me about $4000. When it came to the promotion side of the contract,

Quinn started complaining about spending too much on expenses like advertising, legal fees, and wining and dining the press. Eddie went on and on, crying the blues, until he finally admitted that there would be no profit. There were no earnings for the organization or for my 25% of the promotion, at least until the next fight materialized. He asked me to wait until he promoted his next fight and he would take some money from that deal to pay me what I was owed in terms of the 25%.

After thinking over his explanation, I decided not to fight for Eddie Quinn any longer. I waited until he promoted another fight to see whether I would receive my 25% from the last episode. If I did, that might change my mind. No match was ever made and, as time went on, I knew my decision to break away from Quinn was the right one.

DeMarco, Valenti and Patriarca

Almost two years passed without me having a scheduled fight and I was not breaking any records earning money. Finally, I decided to give it one last shot. I thought that a few more fights meant a few more dollars. I began to train and hoped that I had made the right decision. I realized the end was coming and now, quite frankly, it was strictly fighting for dollars rather than glory.

I trained hard every day for three weeks. Then I received some disturbing news. Rip Valenti was trying to prevent me from fighting. According to my old contract with him, I could only fight at his discretion. I met Lindy at his father's North End smoke shop and asked for his advice. He suggested that I contact someone with clout, someone who could reason with Rip. Lindy also suggested that I fake an injury during my training which would make my contract null and void. I kept that in mind as I went back to the gym to continue my training.

Reporters, managers and fans were waiting for me at the gym. After I worked out with the speed bag and skipped rope, I stopped to wait for Guy Consolo. He was usually on time and apologized for being late. I had two sparring partners waiting to box with me and held them off while I whispered to Guy, "Listen to me, I can't explain it right now, but I'm going to pretend to injure my shoulder. Go along with the charade and I'll explain what's going on later." Guy didn't know what I was up to but went along with what I planned to do.

I climbed in the ring and started sparring with one of my partners, pressing him so I would look good for the first round. When the second round started, I threw one of my left hooks and practically fell with pain as I pretended to hurt my shoulder. Guy jumped in the ring and stopped the sparring match. "That's all," he shouted, "That's all for today." Then, he rushed me to the locker room. After a few minutes, Guy made the announcement that I was injured and would need to see the doctor to determine the seriousness of my injury. We both left the gym and got into my car. I then explained the details of my contract with Valenti that bound me to fight only at his discretion. The contract still had several months left before it expired. Only Valenti could say when and who I would fight. Since I had absolutely no say in the matter, I would have to wait it out. Guy asked what I was going to do. I told him I wasn't sure, but that I needed to speak to someone who was influential enough to help me figure everything out. The only problem was that Rip Valenti knew most everyone in the community. He was well-respected and had a lot of influence. I made a lot of money for a lot of people. At this stage of my career, I felt I was entitled to be totally self-sufficient. I wanted to be in charge of my own destiny for once. If Buccola was around, he'd straighten this mess out.

There was only one man to speak with. I remembered meeting him a while back at promoter John Buckley's office. His name was Raymond Patriarca. The meeting had gone well and he even asked me for an auto-graphed picture. Guy suggested that I contact Mr. Patriarca and explain things to him. After all, Mr. Patriarca was one of the most powerful men in New England. There was only one problem. I didn't know how to get in contact with him, and didn't want to ask the people who might. I thought maybe Benny DeChristoforo might be able to help me. Benny knew a few of the wiseguys in the North End, and could probably make contact for me. I would get in touch with Benny. In the meantime I would keep my arm in a sling, and continue to fake the injury.

The next day, I met Benny at Joe Christy's Luncheonette and explained my problem, as well as my request. He listened attentively and then offered to help. Benny told me he would make contact on my behalf. I thanked him for listening and told me I would appreciate any help he could give. A couple of days later, Benny called to tell me that we had an appoint-ment to meet with Raymond Patriarca at his office in Providence, Rhode

Island. As Benny drove the thirty miles to Providence, we discussed our approach for the meeting with Mr. Patriarca. We arrived to find several men standing outside Mr. Patriarca's office, just observing what was going on. When we announced who we were, they escorted us into the inner office where Mr. Patriarca was waiting. He extended his hand for me to shake and I extended mine clutching a Napoleon cigar for him. I believed that this gesture conveyed respect and appreciation.

Patriarca started the conversation by saying he was not directly involved with the boxing scene in either Providence or Boston, but he would listen to my problem and try to come up with a solution. Patriarca lit the cigar and listened to what I had to say. He sat back and stared out of his window, seldom looking at me while I spoke. Occasionally he would look in my direction and then stare in another direction again. It seemed as though he wasn't paying attention but Mr. Patriarca didn't miss a single word I said, no matter where he was looking as I spoke to him. After I explained my position, Patriarca concluded the meeting with very few words, although he did say that he would help. Patriarca called one of his associates into his office and told him to set up a meeting with Rip Valenti and whoever else might be involved in my problem. As we parted company, Mr. Patriarca told us that if we returned for a meeting the next day, the problem would be resolved. We agreed to return the next day, thanked him, and headed back to Boston.

During the return trip, Benny and I talked over everything that happened at the meeting. Mr. Patriarca was a very important and prominent businessman. In Benny's opinion, the fact that he took the time to listen and that he offered to help me as a mediator, looked very promising.

The next morning, we were all there and on time. Everyone brought something for Mr. Patriarca as a token of their respect. One brought biscotti, another cannoli and yet another brought Cuban cigars. Mr. Patriarca invited us to sit down and asked us to keep open minds and hearts as we discussed the situation at hand. He said the purpose of the meeting was to try to arrive at an agreement that would be mutually beneficial to both sides. Rip Valenti began by describing how he had advanced my career through his expertise in the boxing profession. He added that his reputation was impeccable within the industry, a reputation that he was proud of. Rip explained how he first spotted me in 1953, when I was a local fighter

This appeared in a local Boston paper before my fight with Don Jordan. The copy in the box read: "Tony DeMarco, the street singer with the ring in his voice, serenades Don Jordan tonight as the two former welter champs have a go at the Garden."

going nowhere. At that time, I had nothing and was badly managed. Rip was of the opinion that he made me the boxing success that I had become. By my seventh fight for him I was boxing on national television, and now here I was I was trying to dump him. This made me angry. "What about me?" I asked. "I'm the one who sweats and works hard and I'm the one who takes the punches. I've sacrificed my nights and social life in order to stay in shape. And, for the last seven years, I've been a moneymaker for Rip and the promoters. All I want is to fight for a few more years and settle down with a few dollars in my pocket. That's all." I just wanted to do this on my own without anybody taking a cut of the pie. I owed it to myself and my family.

Raymond Patriarca interrupted me at this point. He suggested that I fight my next three fights for Rip, and that I could keep the entire purse. After that, I could fight on my own with no obligations to anyone. No one said a word. Mr. Patriarca then got up from his desk, walked to the door, opened it and excused everyone, thanking us for being present as we exited. I was happy to accept his decision.

Two weeks later, Rip Valenti informed me that Don Jordan would be my opponent in my first fight under this agreement. Jordan had become the welterweight champion of the world by beating Virgil Akins in a unanimous decision in 1958. He lost the title to Benny "Kid" Paret in 1960, in a hard grueling fight.

The DeMarco-Jordan fight was scheduled for December 19, 1961 at the Boston Garden. I did my usual training to prepare and was as ready as I could possibly be when I entered the ring. The first round was about even, but when I came out for the second round I was ready. I hit Jordan with an impressive left uppercut to the body and he sank to the floor for a full count before the round was at the halfway point. The crowd cheered wildly. Their hometown boy was making a comeback and I started it by knocking out an ex-champion in the second round.

It was six days before Christmas, a holiday which was always special to me. By this point in time, I had been married for a few years and I was happy to have some free time so I could spend Christmas with JoAnn and our baby son, Vincent. He had been born prematurely and had some physical issues including asthma, ear problems and allergies. We would eventually have to make some important decisions, because of Vincent's health, that would impact our future as a family.

The Final Battle in the Ring

Right after Christmas, I started training for my next fight. My opponent, Stefan Redl, was a good boxer who would fight anyone and everyone. He particularly enjoyed fighting former champions like me. The fight was set for February 6, 1962 at the Boston Garden.

I trained in my usual way, running along the Charles River and Jamaica Pond. Occasionally, while running, I would get very sentimental. By this time, Pa had passed away, and I sorely missed him. His emotional support during my morning runs kept me focused and on track with my training. Pa was not a physical man, having been burdened with arthritis and a bad heart as he aged, but even in his later years he always made the effort to be with me on my morning runs. Now that he was gone I missed him.

One day, as I was going through my usual training, I experienced a mood swing and a change of attitude. My spirits dipped to the point that I felt like packing it in. I was down, had no energy and felt uneasy. This was how I felt years earlier when Rip Valenti had me examined at the Pratt Diagnostic Hospital in Boston. The hypoglycemia was rearing its ugly head again.

I tried to work through it, but it was becoming more and more difficult to stay focused. For the first time in my career, I found myself training with very little enthusiasm. Guy Consolo noticed that I was not myself and expressed his concern. I told him that I was losing the desire and determination. The fire was going out. Just a few weeks after KOing Jordan, I was losing interest. It was even to the point that I was seriously considering canceling the Redl fight and abandoning my comeback try. Guy told me that if I felt that way, I should call off the fight and quit right now. If it were only that easy. I didn't want to disappoint all the people who were involved with me and needed the money they would make from the fight. I told Guy that if I felt the same way after the fight, I would quit and look for a regular job.

Guy reminded me that after the Akins fight when I had contemplated retirement, there were no jobs. He said this would be no different. I told Guy that I'd leave it to faith and fate. I did ask him to keep the conversation under his hat. He agreed, and I resumed my training the next day.

The sports reporters started to come around to the gym every time I worked out. They were constantly asking me questions about my condition and how I was feeling about the fight as we got closer and closer. I always told them that I was in very good condition and that I thought I could win.

Everyone was pulling for me, and I made everything sound great but, in reality, the desire was gone. It was time to move on. Training was becoming more difficult because of my attitude. I decided to try training at the same gym I had used when I was just getting started as an amateur. This gave me a better feeling, but I was really just going through the motions. I never missed a training day but it just wasn't the same.

The day before the fight, Redl and I went through the formalities of the weigh-in and both made the welterweight division weight requirements. We then posed for publicity photos, as most of the sportswriters from the Boston papers were in attendance. When we were back on the street, Frankie Campbell suggested eating dinner at Bella Napoli, one of my favorite restaurants. Joe "The Boss" Tecce was a colorful restaurateur and always had a story to tell. Although Bella Napoli was known for Italian food, "The Boss" made me a porterhouse steak.

Finally, it was fight time. I was the favorite, and luckily few realized that I really did not want to be there. After the KO of Jordan, very few were betting against the "Flame and Fury of Fleet Street." The sportswriters made it interesting though, reporting that Redl could, in fact, upset me. One pre-fight headline read, "Redl in Condition to Upset the Odds." The press did a great job hyping the upcoming fight. This, no doubt, boosted the number in attendance on fight night. It wasn't the Boston Garden record-breaking number set during my fight with Carmen Basilio, which drew a capacity crowd of almost 13,500 but 7,000 was a good crowd for this fight. Boxing no longer held the same attraction it did in the 1950s when I fought and beat Vincent Martinez and George Araujo at Fenway Park. The attendance also couldn't match the fight I had with Kid Gavilan on October 13, 1956 at the Boston Garden but, this would be my last fight, and it was against a tough scrappy competitor from Hungary. I was satisfied with the turnout.

I told Guy Consolo I intended to end the fight with a KO. I didn't want to delay my retirement any longer so I told him to look for an early round knockout. Guy told me to stay cool and if the opportunity arose, I should go for it. He didn't want me to get wild and throw punches from left field.

I was anxious to get started. I made my way down to the Garden floor with many cheers and wishes for luck coming from the crowd. This was my thirty-first fight at the Boston Garden. When I entered the ring, I acknowledged the loud cheers. These were, after all, my loyal hometown fans. They cheered and yelled as if they knew it was to be my last fight. Fred Russo, the ring announcer, picked up the microphone and spoke with a commanding voice, "Ladieees and gentlemen, this is the main event of the evening." Russo proceeded to introduce Redl and me. After the usual set of instructions, he sent us back to our corners to await the bell for round one. As I headed for my corner, it dawned on me that I had heard that set of instructions at the beginning of every fight for fifteen years, and this would be the last time I would hear them.

The bell rang and my final battle started. I got the best of Redl right from the beginning but, the Hungarian proved to be a very tough competitor. We went back and forth, round after round, but I was wearing him down. During the last round, we got tangled together and both fell to the canvas, something rarely seen with seasoned fighters, especially during a main event. When I was back in my corner, Guy looked at me laughing and said, "Hey pal, you won the fight." I agreed that I was leading but was concerned that I had not yet knocked Redl out. "Yes," Guy answered, "but you put him on the canvas." I smiled, and told him not to quit his day job, because he would never make it as a comedian. Guy put his hand to his ear and said, "Hey, listen to the crowd." I broke my concentration to focus on the crowd for a second and heard them applauding. Guy pointed and said, "Yeah, they're applauding for you." I listened intently. Yes they were cheering for me as if they all knew. Emotions beyond description were bubbling up. Pa, my brother, my family, my friends…they were all here with me tonight in spirit. As the bell sounded to end the final round, I threw my hands up in the air. Sure enough, I won by a decision. I had won my last fight. Redl and I embraced each other, and I told him that he was a great fighter. He thanked me, gave me a hug and wished me the best. The cheering was deafening and it continued as I left the ring with a huge grin on my face. The final battle was over.

Round 10

Old Mr. Boston

I spent the next several days at home resting and thinking about the future. As hard as I tried, I couldn't seem to come up with any ideas about what I would like to do for work. Now that my boxing career was at an end, I had to find something that would allow my family to continue the lifestyle they were accustomed to.

When I finally left the house, I headed to the gym to visit with Joe DeNucci, who was training for his next bout. While there, I ran into Herb Ralby of *The Boston Globe*. He was one of the many local sportswriters I had developed a good rapport with. We watched Joe work out and both agreed that he was very talented. Herb thought that Joe had the potential to go all of the way. He had already beaten Tiger Jones and fought Joey Giardello to a draw. We were both of the opinion that Joe should have won that bout. Before these fights, DeNucci had knocked out Buddy Cochrane and three other opponents. Herb and I concluded that Joe could possibly become a champion. Little did I know at the time that although Joe DeNucci would not become Champ, he would go on to enter politics and become the State Auditor for the Commonwealth of Massachusetts for many years. He would be highly regarded by both parties for his entire political career.

After Ralby asked me about my plans for the future, I told him that I was ready to start looking for a job. He suggested that I get into sales. I had thought of that but wasn't sure it was a profession I would enjoy. At this point I realized I couldn't be too selective. I just needed to make ends meet and support my young family. Herb told me I could make good money in liquor sales. He thought I would be a natural in that business.

Herb knew some people in the business and said he would call them for me. I thanked him and added that I appreciated his help. Herb suggested that we go to Sam Silverman's office right away to make some inquiries. Sam was a boxing promoter who had an office inside the Sully Square Pool Hall. Johnny Buckley also worked out of there. Buckley had been successful managing champions like Jack Sharkey, Andy Callahan, and many other good fighters including the Middleweight Champion of the World, Paul Pender.

Herb decided to bypass the distributors and go right to the source. He picked up a phone and called the Old Mr. Boston Liquor Company. Herb asked for Gene Bline, a friend of his who had been in the liquor industry for many years and knew everyone. When Herb got him on the line, he told Gene that he had a friend with him who had been in the public eye for many years, who was now looking for a nine-to-five job. Then he mentioned my name. Gene's first response was, "As in, the Champ?" Herb said, "Yes, and he's a good friend of mine who recently retired from the ring. Now, he's looking for a good paying job with a future and I was hoping you could make this happen. It's very important to me." Herb was enthusiastic and agreed to help me but added, "You know, in the liquor industry a salesman works on percentage. The more you sell, the more you earn." Herb said that was understood and Gene Bline agreed to contact me within a few days.

About three days later, Herb called to let me know that I had a sales job at Granada Wine and Liquors in Cambridge. I was to go to the Old Mr. Boston wholesale office and speak with Gene Bline personally. During our meeting, Gene told me he had spoken to Lou Berenson, manager of Granada Wine and Liquors and Eddie Laven, the owner of the firm. Lou was a well-known man in the industry with many years of experience. They decided to give me a couple of big accounts and a few small ones. Gene told me I could start at Granada on the following Monday and that I would report to Mr. Berenson. I was very appreciative for this opportunity and assured Mr. Bline that he would have no regrets.

Monday morning could not come soon enough. I was shaved, showered and dressed within twenty minutes of waking up. I went to Granada Wine and Liquors in Cambridge, where I met Lou Berenson. He was a large man who was warm and full of expression when he spoke. Lou told me that he knew how well-known I was throughout the country, especially in the Boston area. He thought there was no reason why I would not succeed in my new job. I was to start out working with another sales representative. That way, I could become familiar with the products and the selling process. Lou's philosophy was for me to sell myself and I would be effective in the industry. He always told his sales force to tell stories about themselves and what they were doing, because by selling themselves, they would sell their product.

Lou introduced me to Larry Wolf, the salesman I was to shadow. Together, we covered one hundred and fifty accounts each week, visiting liquor stores, bars and restaurants throughout the greater Boston area. Many of the accounts on the list were inactive but, within four months, I had reopened most of them for Granada. The job was working out fabulously. I knew many people and would get to meet a lot more.

A few weeks later, I opened another new account north of Boston on Route 1 in Peabody. The Wagon Wheel was a new nightclub owned by Steve Drugas, an entrepreneur who featured big bands at his establishment like Count Basie, Stan Kenton, Woody Herman and many other bands that drew big crowds.

Steve Drugas was the type of guy who took chances in business and he took a chance with me as his liquor supplier from Granada Wines and Liquors. As we got to know each other, we became fast friends. One day, as I was writing up his new liquor order, Steve asked me to be his part-time host at the Wagon Wheel. The offer sounded interesting. After he told me the work schedule I agreed without hesitation, as I realized that it would not interfere with my sales job for Granada.

The club reminded me of the Palladium Ballroom in Hollywood, California, which brought back many good memories of my travels out west with the guys. I loved my new sales job but working at the Wagon Wheel was the frosting on the cake. A few months later, Steve Drugas asked if I'd like to go with him to New York City. He had an opportunity to book Stan Kenton for a mid-summer appearance and had to sign the necessary contracts. Things were really happening for me. I loved every minute of it.

Moving West

Like many people who come from ethnic neighborhoods in large cities, I wanted to experience suburban living. When I was a kid growing up on Fleet Street in Boston's North End, I lived in an apartment building, a very old apartment building. The lawn was one blade of grass growing out of the cement sidewalk right in front of the building's entrance. Now that my son and daughter were growing up, I wanted something better for them than I had experienced as a city kid. Since the rat race associated with the boxing game was behind me, we decided to move out of the city. I was able to purchase a nice single family home in Braintree, a bedroom community located south of Boston.

We enjoyed family life in our adopted community, but our new lifestyle didn't last long. My son Vincent became very ill. Our family physician told my wife, JoAnn, that his problems were caused by allergies along with a serious case of asthma. She decided to consult a doctor who specialized in respiratory problems. He recommended that Vincent should live someplace with a dry climate, like Las Vegas or Phoenix. JoAnn and I agonized over what we should do. After a few weeks, I started to look into job prospects in the liquor industry in both of those cities. My first choice was Las Vegas, which was the most exciting city I had ever been in. I knew people in both cities and decided I would accept the first job offer that came along, so we could move out west as quickly as possible.

Leaving the Boston area would be difficult. Our roots were here. On top of that, I had established a good reputation as a businessman, and I was still treated like a celebrity. My fame as a boxer didn't hurt my opportunities in the liquor business either. As a result, I was doing rather well financially. There were several other considerations that I thought about. I came from a close-knit extended family. Because of that, I had family obligations that would be factors in my decision. My father was gone and my aging mother had lost her sight. Mom lived with my sister Mary who, like me, was a resident of Braintree. Mary and her husband were the first in the family to move to the suburbs. When I decided to move, I picked Braintree to be close to them. Every day on my way to work, I would pick Mom up and bring her to the Fleet Street apartment. The fact that she was blind didn't prevent her from finding her way to the homes of the old neighbors. She felt her way with her hands. It would be difficult to take my mother away from her daily routine but I had Vincent's health to think about.

Our last day in Boston was December 25, 1963. During the holiday season, we visited many friends and family members to say our goodbyes before leaving for Phoenix on the day after Christmas. I still didn't have a job lined up but I had a few leads, and I was optimistic that I would quickly land a good job in Phoenix or Las Vegas.

When we arrived in Arizona, I made several phone calls looking for work, but then decided I should also try my luck in Las Vegas. I thought I should be able to land a sales job there, or even work as a greeter at one of the Vegas casinos. I felt confident that I could handle the glamour, excitement and lifestyle of that city. As 1964 rapidly approached, the economy was at a standstill and it wasn't as easy to find a job as I thought it would be. After a few days in Vegas without turning up any good prospects, I returned to Phoenix. Luckily, one of the calls I made when we first arrived paid off. I was contacted by a liquor company that was interested in speaking with me. I set up an appointment with Mr. Childs of the True Childs Distributing Company, a liquor distributor that carried the same products that I sold in Boston.

Mr. Childs reminded me of an old Boston Yankee, warm in many ways but strictly business. He seemed impressed by my resume and very interested in my boxing years. He wanted to hire me as a salesman and public relations representative, but he had no openings at that time. Mr. Childs did say he expected an opening to develop in the near future, so he would keep me in mind. I was very interested in the position and eagerly suggested that if Mr. Childs would give me the company's dead accounts, I would turn them around and reactivate them. I guaranteed it.

I had to return to Boston to tie up some loose ends, and told Mr. Childs I would be available to start when I returned to Phoenix in six weeks. He complimented me on my spirit and promised there would be a job waiting for me when I got back from Boston.

Las Vegas just wasn't in the cards for me, but Phoenix was a vibrant, rapidly growing city, and the weather usually wasn't hard to take either. Our first experience with the Phoenix weather wasn't a great one though. When we arrived late Christmas night, it was raining, which had a bad affect on Vincent. He began to wheeze so badly that we rushed him to the local hospital for an allergy shot. We all hoped that the weather would improve, so Vincent would get better.

Not long after we arrived, we looked up Steve and JoAnn Catalanotto, friends from the North End, who had moved to Phoenix before us. Like Vincent, they had medical problems which prompted their move west. Steve had asthma and JoAnn had polio, but they didn't let that interfere with their everyday life. Along with their daughter Christen, they had opened a restaurant in Phoenix and worked long hours to make their establishment a success. They assured us the rain was a rarity and the weather would quickly improve. Having friends nearby from back home made us feel a little more secure in our new surroundings.

My daughter Sylvia was just a toddler when we moved, and thankfully was in the best of health. I felt bad that, due to Vincent's health, she sometimes took a back seat, but she was an ideal child and never complained. When I went back to Boston, JoAnn and the kids stayed in Phoenix at our new apartment which was close to the Catalanotto's restaurant and home. I felt comfortable about leaving my family because I knew that friends were nearby, just in case.

On that flight back to Boston, I worried constantly about Vincent and his health problems. I wasn't sure I had done the right thing by moving my family to Phoenix. I kept telling myself that my son needed a dry climate and that was all that mattered.

Although there were many loose ends to take care of before I could return to Phoenix, the most important was to sell our apartment in the North End. This would be a challenge not only because January is not a great time of the year to sell property in New England, but also because there was a real estate slump in the greater Boston market. What made things worse was the demise of the West End, the neighborhood next to the North End. The entire West End had just become the victim of politicians and developers who wanted to tear down the old tenements, sell some of the property to the nearby Massachusetts General Hospital, and build luxury apartments with the land that was left over. Even though neighborhood groups lobbied and protested, the West End lost out. The city took it over by eminent domain in the 1960s and tore down all the tenements, dispossessing the families that lived there. I had heard that the developers would set their sights on the North End next, and was afraid

Posing with two of the greats, Mickey Walker and Paul Pender.

that no one would want to buy in my old neighborhood.

At that point I decided it probably would be a lot easier to rent my apartment than to try and sell it. I asked my friend and former schoolmate, Ronnie Cassesso, if he knew anybody who would be interested in renting my apartment. I was in luck. Ronnie told me that he had just the right person in mind, a friend of his who would be good for the $125 per month rent that I was looking for.

Before leaving for Phoenix, I went to the Wagon Wheel to visit Steve Drugas. He was glad to see me and told me that if ever I decided to return, he'd have a job waiting for me. As soon as I got back to Phoenix, I got in touch with Mr. Childs. He was as good as his word, and I started work right away. His sales strategy seemed to be the same as Granada's. I was set up with contacts that were tied to boxing or sports in general.

The geographical layout of the streets in Phoenix was very easy to learn. Because it was a newer city, the streets were planned as a grid, with everything at right angles. The west side streets were numbered avenues. The east side thoroughfares were numbered streets. Low numbered streets ran south and high numbered streets ran north. The middle of the avenues and streets were divided by Central Avenue and the middle of the south and north was divided by Camelback Road. This was much easier than Boston, and I learned the layout of the city rather quickly. I was given one hundred accounts in the city and was able to cover all of them in a short period of time. The fifty located in the suburbs took me a little longer.

Anyone who can navigate through Boston can navigate anywhere with no problem. Boston is such an old city that the streets started out as cow paths. When the streets were paved in the late 1800s, the city just paved over the original pathways. As a result, there is no rhyme or reason for most of Boston's streets. You have to live there to be able to understand the illogic and navigate. Some Bostonians who have lived in the city all of their lives still get lost. The layout began in 1630. That was a long time ago.

As the months passed, I had great success and won many sales contests. The weather in Phoenix during March, April and May was very comfortable. When June, July and August came around we suffered with the heat. It was intense. Temperatures hit from 100 degrees to 110 degrees almost every day. With that kind of heat, I couldn't even touch the steering wheel to drive, making my line of work pretty uncomfortable in the summer. The one good thing about the dry heat was the positive impact it had on Vincent's respiratory condition. His asthma seemed to be improving with the Arizona climate.

Tony DeMarco's Living Room

Even though I was successful in my sales job, I decided to look for other business opportunities. The nightclub business had always intrigued me, and I thought that I could really do well in a business that I knew I would love. I asked around to see if any of my new friends knew of an available location. As fate would have it, I heard about a place from a most unlikely source, our baby sitter, Dorothy Ginsberg. She had heard about a lounge that might be up for sale. I visited the good looking but badly managed cocktail lounge that was owned by two brothers, Charles and Harold Gannon. Called the Silver Poodle, it was located at 40th Street and

Camelback Road, just a stones-throw from the upscale suburb of Scottsdale. This was a prime location for just about any business, but it was ideal for a cocktail lounge.

I began negotiations with the Gannon brothers and we haggled back and forth for some time. Finally they agreed to my compromise price and I bought the Silver Poodle. I had plans to develop the place into a sophisticated nightspot, not as glamorous as what you might experience in Las Vegas, but it would be a classy local lounge with live music.

I had been around long enough as a lounge host and a liquor salesman to see the potential in this venue. I couldn't wait to tell my good friend, Jim Spero, about my new venture. Jim was a talented radio personality, possibly one of the best in the business. I met him in 1963 and we quickly became close friends. I listened to Jim on the radio every morning at home, and also during my business stops. Right from the beginning, he encouraged my efforts as a salesman. Jim was there for me when I was thinking about buying the Silver Poodle Lounge and also later on, when the deal was consummated. One thing that impressed me about Jim was the fact that he kept himself in great physical shape. He not only liked sports and athletics, but he was involved himself. He played golf and lifted weights.

The Silver Poodle definitely needed a new identity. I thought about Peter Fiumara's place in Boston called The Living Room. It was located on Stuart Street in the downtown area and was warm, comfortable, and intimate. I liked the atmosphere in Peter's place and loved the intimacy of the name. I decided to try to duplicate that concept and Tony DeMarco's Living Room was born.

I decorated the club with photographs of myself with some top celebrities that I hung behind the piano bar. My championship belt was placed over the cash register so patrons could also view the belt from the bar area. I updated the club with indirect lighting and had a special spotlight placed in the ceiling over the piano bar. This light had a dimmer switch for effect and atmosphere. The entertainers would be able to control the lighting effects they wanted with a push of a button. The decor and the lighting ended up being just what I had envisioned. The slogan that I created for advertising the club was "Where Good People Meet."

My careful planning paid off and the lounge clicked immediately. I brought in live entertainment every night including Sundays. This was in

The Nightclub Owner.

contrast to most of the other clubs in Phoenix that closed late Saturday night and didn't reopen until Monday evening. I called Sunday evenings "Celebrity Night at The Living Room." Entertainers like Laura Lee, Emilio Flame, and Don Breault played the piano and the customers would sing along. Surprisingly, there were always a lot of good voices in the room, waiting to sing their favorite songs. The entertainers generally had their own following which added to the crowd that came to try out their voices. My favorite pianist was Emilio Flame. When I listened to his stylish offerings, it reminded me of Carmen Cavalero, a great pianist in his day.

In the late 1960s, a new type of music was gaining popularity throughout the nightclub circuit. Pop music sung by solo acoustic guitarists became very popular and I decided to hire Michael Urias, a talented local musician who had a big following. He was handsome and a bit flamboyant which, when combined with his talent, made him a popular attraction at The Living Room.

One weekend, I took Michael to Las Vegas so he could experience the music scene there. Sonny King was appearing at the side lounge at the Sands Hotel and I decided we should take in his show. I introduced Michael to Sonny, who then asked him to perform a few of his songs. The crowd loved Michael's performance. They applauded for so long that Sonny gave Michael an encore. As an up-and-coming young entertainer, Michael gained a lot of confidence and stage presence from this experience.

Even though it was a neighborhood lounge, The Living Room began to attract some great personalities. One day Charlie Pride walked in, sat down, ordered a drink, and just wanted to relax. He was accompanied by someone I knew slightly, George Joyce, a bartender at a local Phoenix hotel. George had suggested The Living Room as a nice relaxing place to go for a drink. Charlie Pride was congenial and accommodating and even agreed to sing a few of his many hits for my customers. Broderick Crawford, a popular television actor, also visited The Living Room quite a bit. Crawford's gravelly voice and mannerisms reminded me of my friend Joe Coppola from the North End. I once told Crawford about Joe, explaining how I thought they were so much alike. He smiled and said, "Good lookin' guy, huh?"

I tried to give the public the entertainment they wanted, and hired Harry Charles, a singer/guitarist who had composed the popular song, "I Want the Best for You." He performed at The Living Room longer than any other entertainer. Harry also had the largest repertoire of any singer I ever hired. He could sing and play for an entire evening and never repeat a tune. Many performers will use the same material from the earlier part of the evening's performance when they play their last show of the night. Chances are that the audience has changed, having turned over once or twice during the evening. The late crowd wouldn't know they were hearing a repeat of the earlier show. Harry was unique as each set or show was different from the one before.

**

The winter of 1965 was the last time the Boston Red Sox spent their training season in Scottsdale, Arizona. Most of the major league teams that were not already located in Florida for pre-season training were now heading southeast to the Sunshine State. This was a bad break for me because The Living Room was a favorite hangout of many of the Red Sox players and front office staff. This was the last training season for them in Scottsdale and I was determined make the best of it.

A young slugger from Revere, a city just north of Boston, showed up for pre-season training that year. The buzz was that Tony Conigliaro was the best thing to happen to the Red Sox since they signed Ted Williams. We were introduced one evening at The Living Room and we hit it off right from the start. I discovered that Tony was not only an up-and-coming ballplayer, but he also loved to sing. Tony "C" entertained at the lounge whenever he was in the mood. I venture to say that if he had not chosen baseball, he could have had a career in show business as a lounge singer.

Ted Williams and I had been friends for some time. He was a boxing fan and if I had a match in Boston when he and the Sox were in town, Ted would be ringside. I developed a similar relationship with Tony "C," who in his first season in the major leagues, made the sports fans sit up and take notice. In his first time at the plate in a Red Sox uniform, he swung at the first pitch and hit a home run. If it hadn't been for a tragic accident that occurred in 1967, he would likely have been a Hall of Famer. Tony was hit in the face with an inside pitch that affected his vision. Once he recuperated he was back in the lineup but his eyesight was never the same, and it was all downhill from that point on. Tony was a nice kid who didn't deserve a break like that. He should have had a long and brilliant career in professional baseball.

***

The atmosphere was just right and the entertainment was terrific, making The Living Room a very successful lounge. A big help was the continuous boosting I received from Jim Spero. His constant support began in the 1960s and continued through the early 1980s. Quite often, Jim invited me to be a guest analyst on his radio program. When there was a sporting event worth speaking about publicly, especially a scheduled fight, Jim called on me for my analysis. One of the most talked about fights in the heavyweight division was the Ali-Frazier match, which took place on March 8, 1971.

Prior to the fight, I accepted Jim's invitation to speak on his show and, as usual, the subject turned to boxing. Much to Jim's surprise, I picked "Smoking" Joe Frazier to defeat the favorite, Muhammed Ali. I picked Frazier because of his punching ability. He had KO'd fighters and in the process had demonstrated unbeatable footwork, shuffling in on his opponents in a better way than Ali, who was famous for his excellent footwork.

Jim Spero disagreed with my prediction wholeheartedly and we good-naturedly argued our opinions on the upcoming Ali-Frazier fight. Finally, we provoked each other into an extravagant wager. The winner of the wager would receive a handmade Italian silk designer necktie purchased by the loser.

As the day of the fight arrived, Jim was confident he would be wearing that new designer necktie before midnight. This was the first of what would become a series of three Ali-Frazier fights. Late that night, as I tied the knot in my winner's necktie, I smiled knowing the experts were wrong. I had predicted Joe Frazier as the winner and I was right.

***

One of the great pleasures in my life occurred when the Boston Celtics came to Phoenix and played the Suns in basketball. Whenever they competed against each other, the legendary voice of the Boston Celtics, Johnny Most, would stop by to visit with me at the lounge. He always took the time to visit, no matter how busy his schedule was. I met Johnny for the first time years earlier when he first came to Boston to do the radio broadcasts of the Celtics games. I remember the time Herb Ralby and Johnny Most visited me at my family home on Fleet Street and my parents treated them to homemade biscotti with anisette flavored coffee.

Johnny always made himself at home when he visited me at The Living Room. On several occasions, he brought along the Celtics former star and current head coach Tom Heinsohn. Tom was a real gentleman. The two were good friends and were often seen together when the team was on the road. In his later years, Johnny's health failed to the point that he could no longer broadcast the Celtics games. Johnny retired and was confined to a wheel chair. One of the last times I saw him was at an Italian American Sports Hall of Fame banquet at Lombardo's in Randolph, Massachusetts. Johnny was one of the guests that evening. I was disappointed

The DeMarco Family with Sonny King and Jimmy Durante.

to see that he was still smoking cigarettes and it looked as if the end was near. Unfortunately, it was. Within weeks of the event, he was gone.

As the years passed and The Living Room became well-known, more and more celebrities dropped by when they were in town. I couldn't have made a go of it without the support of the locals though. I always appreciated the support of two local celebrities; wrestler Lou Thesz and former lightweight champion Lou Ambers. Their patronage helped make The Living Room a local destination, and kept my business strong.

Even though I was successful in Phoenix, I still continued to dream about Las Vegas. I visited there as often as I could, not only for the entertainment, but also to see my many friends who lived there year round, and other friends from Los Angeles who frequented Vegas. Our good friends from Boston who were close neighbors in Phoenix, Steve and JoAnn Catalanotto, ended up moving to Las Vegas, so I always connected with them when I was in town.

Another friend I reconnected with in Vegas was Al Siciliano. We were friends as kids, but lost touch when he joined the Marines as a young man. He was stationed in San Diego, and instead of coming home to the North End when he was discharged, he stayed in California. Al became a police officer in Los Angeles. When he retired from the LAPD, he took a top security position for the Tropicana Hotel in Las Vegas. Al also became very active in the fight scene in Las Vegas, working as a boxing judge and even boxing in exhibition bouts. In that capacity, he battled with some of the former boxing champions who were passing through the area, including yours truly.

***

After a few years of operating The Living Room, I believed the next step to our financial security would be to buy the land on which the lounge was built. I approached the owner, Charles Gilerland, with a very reasonable offer for the property in 1968. His counter offer was out of my price range, but I have to admit it was in line with the land prices which had escalated significantly by then.

As time went on, I continued to do well at The Living Room. The one major problem was the cost of entertainment, which kept going up. I had to offset this expense by increasing the cost of drinks proportionately. This works out fine as long as there are no unforeseen problems. Unfortunately, I became the recipient of a major problem. The city began a project to repair and update the water pipes and natural gas lines.

Most of the work on this project would take place right in front of The Living Room, and was projected to take eighteen months to complete. No matter how popular my lounge was, after eighteen months my patrons would surely find new favorite spots to hang out. Not only was this a tremendous financial loss to me, but I also lost out on buying the land. To add insult to injury, Charles Gilerland sold the land to the U-Haul Company, right under my nose. There I was with three years left on the lease, and no way for my patrons to get to me. I looked for a new location nearby but had no luck.

There were no apologies from the "Sunny City," as they set up traffic detours in the immediate area that made it almost impossible to get to the lounge. The construction would slow business down for almost a year and a half. As revenues dropped, I had to dip into my savings to stay in business. When my own money ran out, I had to take out loans just to pay my bills and make ends meet.

"A friend in need is a friend indeed," as the saying goes. Anyway, a friend came to my rescue. Sonny King called me to tell me that he would be in Phoenix for a two-day engagement at the Playboy Club, subbing for an entertainer who canceled out last minute. A couple of days later, Sonny arrived and was shocked to see how difficult it was to get to The Living Room. He had planned to make an appearance at the lounge but considering the circumstances, insisted on appearing on my stage after each of his shows at the Playboy Club. Actually, the Playboy Club was located in downtown Phoenix, on Central Avenue, about fifteen minutes from The Living Room. Sonny's schedule was tight but he was determined to help his old friend. He even announced his late night show at The Living Room during each of his shows at the Playboy Club. Sonny told patrons that they would have to walk to The Living Room, because there was no access to the street due to construction. He seemed like the proverbial Pied Piper, taking his following with him right through my front door.

I called many of my regular customers to let them know Sonny would be appearing, and also asked Jim Spero if he would plug it on his morning radio show. Sonny's appearance at The Living Room was a great success. People went out of their way to walk to the lounge to see Sonny and showed their appreciation with cheers, applause and requests for autographs. Sonny King was a big hit and I was proud that he had appeared at my club.

Before he returned to Las Vegas, Sonny stopped by the house to see my family and chat over a cup of coffee. The subject of dogs came up as we were all pet lovers. He mentioned that an acquaintance of his knew of a litter of Schnauzers, ready to be born. The pups would soon be up for sale. A breeder in Vegas let the word go out that a dog owned by one of her best customers was expecting any day. The customer turned out to be Vido Musso. I had met Vido when I was last in Vegas. At that time the tenor sax player was appearing with Louis Prima and Keely Smith. He had a reputation of being one of the better jazz musicians on the West Coast, having starred with the Stan Kenton Orchestra when he first came from Italy. He had the amazing ability to hear a song or arrangement once and memorize it on the spot.

The Schnauzer pup was a good excuse for me to visit Las Vegas for a few days. When I returned home to Phoenix, I brought Vita with me, a cute little female pup from the litter Sonny told us about. She was an instant hit with the family.

***

Although business suffered, we survived. Soon after the city's water project was completed, things got back to normal and The Living Room was as popular as ever. On the night of Saturday, June 14, 1975, Michael Urias was playing his guitar to a packed house when I was called to the phone. The call was from a Tony Liotta from Brooklyn, New York. He traveled all over the country with his job as a salesman. In each town, he would look in the local phone directories for the name Liotta in hopes that he might find some long lost relatives.

When he arrived in Phoenix, he found the name Leonardo Liotta and decided to call. I was usually referred to as Tony DeMarco but was listed in the phone book by my real name. After I said hello, he said, "Is this Mr. Liotta?" When I said that it was he added, "Well, this is Mr. Liotta." I started to laugh and he explained his little hobby. Later, he dropped by the lounge and for the first time in my life, I met someone outside my family with the same last name. As we spoke, we tried to determine if we were related to each other somewhere down the line.

I brought Tony Liotta home to meet my family and share a few laughs. My children heard the car as the two Liottas pulled in the driveway. Vincent and Sylvia ran out of the house to greet me. It was a great introduction for Tony Liotta to the DeMarco family.

You may ask why two people with the same last name made such a big deal of meeting each other. If the names were common Anglo names like Smith or Jones, I don't think Tony Liotta would have bothered with his hobby. Italian surnames are generally common to only a province or town in Italy. For example, Liotta is common in just a couple of Sicilian towns. Last names like Lombardo, DiNapoli, or Valentino would be common to a larger area in Italy, but not spread all over the country like Jones or Smith might be in England. This means that two Americans with the same Italian last names might possibly be related with parents, grandparents or distant cousins from the same province in Italy.

A Father's Day That Changed My Life

It was a beautiful Sunday morning in June when my son, Vincent, woke me up holding a cup of coffee in his hands. He smiled, handed me the coffee and said, "Wake up, it's Father's Day." If that wasn't enough, he and my daughter, Sylvia, had shined every pair of my shoes. An even bigger Father's Day surprise was obvious when I walked into the kitchen a bit later. Vincent was making spaghetti sauce, supervised by his mother. Of course, we never called it "sauce". It was always called "gravy" in my family. Our two favorite kinds of gravy were *Bolognese* (with meat) or *Marinara* (meatless). Pasta in my family was called macaroni. So while others might have sauce on their pasta, we enjoyed gravy on our macaroni.

That evening, after we dined on Vincent's macaroni and gravy, he decided to ride his bike to the local 7-Eleven store, which was about a tenth of a mile from our house. He wanted to buy something and said he wouldn't be gone long. I waited patiently for his return as we were in the middle of a chess game. Vincent had learned to play the game at school, loved it, and was quite good at it.

Time passed and there was no sign of my son. I was getting concerned. The store was just down the street. He should have been back long before. It was eight o'clock in the evening but still daylight, so I decided to wait just a little longer before going out to look for him. I thought he might have been delayed by some neighborhood friends. Just then, I heard a siren in the distance but didn't think much about it. It never occurred to me that it could have anything to do with Vincent's absence. As time went on I started to imagine the worst. What if Vincent had fallen off his new bicycle? I shook the thought off, saying to myself that my nerves were allowing my imagination to run wild.

A short time later, one of our neighbors knocked on my door. Mrs. O'Connor, who lived three houses away, came to tell us that Vincent had been in an accident. My wife JoAnn and I rushed to the accident scene. Once we got there, we were advised to go to the Scottsdale Hospital. Another neighbor drove us to the hospital as both JoAnn and I were too emotional to drive. It seemed to take forever to get there. Sylvia, who was twelve at the time stayed home alone, watching an old Dean Martin and Jerry Lewis movie.

When we finally arrived at the hospital, we were met by the attending

My dear son, Vincent.

doctor who informed us that Vincent was hit while riding his bicycle. The doctor told us Vincent was seriously injured and may not survive the accident. He said it was possible Vincent would have serious medical problems and that he could potentially end up in a permanent vegetative state. Hearing this, JoAnn yelled out, "Then may God take him now."

The doctor returned to the emergency room to attend to Vincent. It was not long before he came back, shaking his head saying, "Vincent did not suffer long." Our wonderful boy, whose life was so full of promise, was now just a spirit. My boy was only fourteen years old. At that moment, my whole life changed forever.

The next day, Officer Grant of the police department stopped by our house to extend his condolences. He took the time to explain what took place to JoAnn and me, describing how the driver of the car that hit Vincent was speeding, trying to beat the light at the corner near the 7-Eleven. As drivers of the other cars at the intersection came to a stop, this one car sped up. Vincent was in his path, and he hit him straight on. The driver didn't have any auto insurance and, ironically, was a law student studying for the bar exam.

I was in shock over the sudden loss of my dear son, Vincent. The reality of the loss hit me hard on the next day, but I pulled myself together to make the funeral arrangements. I was exhausted from lack of sleep, and was functioning solely on nervous energy. When it came time to choose a casket for my son, I almost fell apart. As soon as he could get away from his radio show, Jim Spero stayed right by my side the whole time. He helped me handle all of the funeral arrangements that day, including lining up Michael Urias to play guitar at the wake. At the wake, I was very touched by the number of friends, family, and even strangers, who came to the funeral home to share our loss.

Twenty-six years earlier, my brother Andrew had passed away. The similarities overwhelmed me. It happened on the same day of the week, Sunday, and at exactly the same time, eight o'clock in the evening. I had been watching "The Dean Martin and Jerry Lewis Show" on television with my friends, Smeaky Pasquale and Dominic DiGiovanni, when I learned of the death of my brother.

Andrew and Vincent were both fourteen years old when they died. There were other similarities between Andrew and my son Vincent. Both had been sickly most of their lives and both died at exactly the same time on a Sunday evening in June. I was watching Dean Martin and Jerry Lewis on television when my brother died. When Vincent died, my daughter Sylvia was also watching Martin and Lewis.

My thoughts then traveled to the older brother I never knew. Leonardo died in 1931, when my mother was pregnant with me. After the sad loss of their firstborn son, my parents decided to name me Leonardo, in his memory. I have always wished that I had the opportunity to know my brother Nardo.

JoAnn and I decided that Vincent should be laid to rest in Boston where he was born. Even though we had been in Phoenix for many years, Boston was still home. Our relatives and closest friends lived in the city and nearby communities and we both needed their emotional support. I called a friend, Jim Sanders, a supervisor for American Airlines, who made the arrangements for us to bring Vincent back to Boston for burial. The funeral mass was held at the Sacred Heart Church in the North End. After the service, we buried our son in St. Michael's Cemetery in Roslindale, a suburban section of Boston.

Having the support of family and friends was comforting in our time of loss, so we decided to stay on in Boston for a while. We were sur-rounded by our family and closest friends which helped us a great deal. It is very difficult to write about the loss of one's child. Why things like this happen we will never really know. I do know that my boy Vincent is in a very special place, the place some people call Heaven.

Trying to Get on with Life

After the death of our son, it was very difficult to deal with the day to day activities that went on in our lives. I was severely depressed and had a hard time staying focused. After several months passed, I received a call one day from an Arizona boxing promoter. He wanted to hire me to referee a preliminary boxing match. Arizona's Reuben Castillo was the main event and the referee for that bout was to be none other than former heavyweight champion, Joe Louis. I discussed the offer with JoAnn, who encouraged me to accept it. We both agreed it would be good for me to be busy again. I flew back to Arizona to take care of business, while JoAnn and my twelve-year-old daughter Sylvia stayed on in Boston with the family.

Many years earlier, Joe Louis had boxed in an exhibition match against Johnny Shkor at the Boston Garden. I was also on the card at the Garden on the night of November 14, 1949, slated to box Frankie Steele (Stellato), a local scrapper.

Steele had been a champion boxer for the U.S. Marines and as two Bostonians, we had become good friends. We attended many of the same social functions and spent a lot of time together. After the fight was an-nounced, we deliberately avoided each other. The fight turned out to be a real brawl. Frankie had the experience but I had toughness and endurance. It was a close battle, but I won by decision. Frankie and I had a rematch later on. Fortunately, I was very prepared for the match won by a knockout.

Frankie and I often spoke about the honor of fighting on the same card as Joe Louis, the longest reigning heavyweight champion of the world. Now I was honored to be a referee at the same event as Louis.

It felt very strange to head back to Phoenix alone, leaving JoAnn and Sylvia behind in Boston. Being back in Phoenix brought the pain of Vin-cent's loss back at full force. My friends, particularly those at The Living Room, were very supportive and understanding, but they couldn't heal my loss. I began drinking more heavily, because the booze helped to numb the emotional pain that I was going through. I became severely depressed and even felt that I was losing my focus on what was right and wrong.

As often as I could, I escaped to Las Vegas to drink, gamble and carouse. Thankfully, Al Siciliano kept my life in check. We would talk for hours about life, family, the old days and dealing with loss. Al suggested that I get involved in some of the boxing exhibitions in Las Vegas. He thought that it would be like the good old days when I boxed with Smeaky Pasquale and the rest of my buddies. I decided to give it some thought.

Sicily

I needed to find a way to reconnect with JoAnn and Sylvia. The loss of our son certainly put a strain on our relationship. I thought a trip might do us some good after our tragic loss, and decided Italy should be our destination. Sciacca, Sicily appealed to me as it was the city Mom and Pa came from, and I had never been there. A bustling port city noted for it's fishing industry, Sciacca later became famous for the luxury resorts that attract tourists from around the world. JoAnn agreed that it was a good idea to get away, so we packed our bags and off we went.

In Palermo, Sicily with Phil Buccola.

On the way to Sciacca, we stopped in Palermo to visit with Phil Buccola who had returned to his birthplace some years earlier. Rip Valenti had given me his address. Phil was a well-respected businessman who, at this point in time, was a man in his eighties. When he saw me, he gave me a warm and gracious welcome, Italian style. That means, a handshake and a kiss on each cheek, followed by a bear hug. Phil gave me the tour of his home and then asked if I would like to see Palermo. As we walked the streets of the city, we spoke about what had happened with my New York contract and what could have happened. Phil gave Rip Valenti a lot of credit for his success with the contract negotiations, which took place just after Phil returned to Italy.

Phil mentioned that, if things had gone a little differently in the early days, he would have loved to promote me. Phil told me he thought the management team of his nephew Dick Horgan and Johnny Buckley would have brought me great success. In retrospect, I think that it was better that I did not box for the boys from Providence and Boston. I did okay, better than most, the route that I went.

When I told Phil that I had planned to visit my mother's side of the family in Sciacca that day, he immediately got on the phone with his personal driver. Phil was kind enough to arrange for his driver to take us to Sciacca which was about 100 miles away from Palermo.

It was a great experience to visit our "roots" in Sicily, meeting distant family members and renewing old friendships. We returned to Phoenix in much better spirits, but in our case, time did not heal all wounds.

Round 11

A New Beginning

Parents who have lost children are sometimes drawn closer, but more often, they end up drifting apart from one another. For two years after we lost Vincent, JoAnn and I tried unsuccessfully to keep the marriage going. We both worked hard to get on with life, but in the end, the anxiety and pressure of our loss could not be overcome. Eventually we separated. I made the decision to move out, and rented an apartment with a friend of mine, Jim Sanders, who was also having some marital difficulties. We chose an apartment in a new complex on the south end of 40th Street, close to The Living Room.

One evening several months later, I was behind the bar listening to Harry Charles strum his guitar and softly sing a medley of love songs. The music had put me in a mellow mood when in walked Linda Yarsheda. She immediately caught my eye. It seemed that we couldn't stop staring at each other. I just couldn't resist approaching her, so I introduced myself and we chatted for a bit. Because it seemed that the interest was mutual, we spent several hours enjoying cocktails and getting to know each other. Linda was Scandinavian on her mother's side and Japanese on her father's. Her father was a military man, an army officer who had brought Linda and the family to live in many fascinating places. Wherever he was stationed, his family was with him. This made Linda a world traveler with many stories to share about the United States and foreign lands. For that period of time, Linda became an escape from the turmoil that surrounded my life. Right or wrong, I needed a diversion, and Linda became that diversion. My partying lifestyle kicked into high gear.

Rocky's Hideaway, owned by Rock Castanza, was one of my favorite

Posing in The Living Room with the personally autographed picture Sinatra sent after we met in Las Vegas.

restaurants because I was treated like royalty, it was close to home, and the Porterhouse steaks were the best in the west. Rocky was well-known and well-liked. In addition to being the proprietor, he was a musician, and seemed to prefer playing the piano to running the restaurant. As far as I was concerned, Rocky's Hideaway was a one-of-a-kind restaurant, and I loved it. If Rocky was at the piano when I walked in, he would start playing "Body and Soul," a tune from an old John Garfield movie, because he thought I resembled Garfield. Linda Yarsheda felt very comfortable in Rocky's and the attention I received didn't hurt my image.

The partying got more intense with the booze continuously flowing. Linda and I thought nothing of traveling from Phoenix to Vegas at the drop of a hat. We saw just about every show that Las Vegas had to offer. I often dropped in on my pal, Sonny King, who was a mainstay with Jimmy Durante. Wayne Newton had a thing for pretty women and whenever we were in his company, he seemed captivated by Linda. One night I was in his dressing room after his show and he inquired about Linda. I basically looked him in the eye and said, "Not available." He got the message and changed the subject. My radical lifestyle change continued, as I became very comfortable with the glitz and glamour of Vegas, and show business in general.

Being a well-known former Champion, I often found myself in the company the stars that played the Strip in Vegas such as Joey Bishop, the guys from the late Louis Prima's band and his widow, the singer Keely Smith. One evening I ran into Sammy Davis Jr. and reminisced about his guest appearance as a commentator for my televised fight with Carmen Basilio on Rocky Marciano's television show. Sammy nodded and said the he would never forget that fight. He called it one of the greatest battles he had ever seen. He invited me to see his show at the Sands Hotel and as I watched him, I realized that he was one of the world's greatest entertainers. He could do it all: sing, dance, tell stories, joke and even play a couple of instruments. He was truly one of a kind.

One of the highlights of this period in my life was being invited to a private party being thrown by the Chairman of the Board, Frank Sinatra. I was at the Riviera, talking to Eliot Price, a major stockholder of the hotel and manager of the casino. Eliot personally invited me because Sinatra was a huge boxing fan. Sinatra greeted us at the door of his suite and was a gracious host. It was a most memorable evening as I had a lengthy conversation with the Chairman of the Board that night. I was touched when Sinatra later sent me a picture of himself which I proudly displayed in The Living Room.

Willie the Godson

Willie Fopiano was born in the North End just like I was, but we never met in the old neighborhood. He was quite a bit younger than me and was still just a teenager when I moved to Phoenix. Years later, we met when I was in Las Vegas with Al Siciliano. Al introduced us, and when we heard each other's names we realized we had quite a few mutual friends.

Floppy, as he was known to many of his friends, worked in Las Vegas operating junkets between Boston and Vegas. At that point in his life, he had already written his autobiography entitled "The Godson."

After Floppy made a few phone calls, my accommodations were changed to a lavish suite at the Frontier Hotel. Three days of fun at the hotel were simply an understatement, that is, if I didn't think about the gambling debts I incurred while I was there. Floppy was quite the character. As it turned out he had always dreamed of being a boxer, but he became sidetracked with gambling, robbery, and the wiseguy mentality.

When Floppy checked in to make sure I was having a good time, I assured him I was having a great time. I loved Las Vegas and the lifestyle that allowed me to unwind every time I ventured there. When he asked how I was doing with Lady Luck, I admitted that I had lost quite a bit of money. Floppy suggested I might be better off if I forgot about the gambling and just focused on having fun. To have a fighting chance at the tables, I really needed to learn the intricacies of whatever game I was playing. I decided to listen to Floppy and back off from the haphazard way I was trying to get rich at the gambling tables. After all, no one breaks the bank. Casinos make millions a day from guys just like me who gamble without knowing the finer points of the games. I suddenly realized I had been literally throwing my money away, and decided to stop gambling before I got into serious financial trouble.

Years later, after I saw the movie, "Casino" with Robert DeNiro, I thought about Floppy, the good time in Las Vegas, and my attempts at gambling. I realized, in retrospect, that I had made the right decision by backing off. I just wasn't cut out to be a gambler.

Two Different Worlds

My lady friend, Linda Yarsheda went home to California to visit her family in Los Angeles. I was still running back and forth between Phoenix and Las Vegas. It was a busy time at The Living Room, but I made the time to enjoy myself in the gambling capital of the world.

When Linda returned to Phoenix, she seemed different. She said, "Los Angeles was nice, but I like what I have here." With pen in hand, she sketched a rather intimate, if not bawdy, picture of me. I was taken back at what she drew, so I just smiled and told her that she was a nut. She replied, "I might be a nut, honey, but if you're nice, I'll share a joint with you." I didn't think it was a good idea as I had never tried marijuana. Linda said that she had picked up some "stuff" in Los Angeles. She claimed that it was called Columbian Gold and that it was the best you could buy. Maybe I came across as a naïve bumpkin, but I was not too interested. I had never experienced any type of drug that wasn't prescribed by a physician. Anyway, I told Linda that I might try a hit or two of her joint before I left for The Living Room.

Actually, I took the joint with me and several hours later, just before I was ready to leave the club, I decided to try a few puffs of what looked to me like a hand-rolled cigarette. I didn't feel anything, and couldn't see what was so great about it. A short time later while I was still at the lounge, the marijuana started to take effect. What made things worse was that my normally sharp, dependable bartender, David, wasn't feeling well and asked me to cover for him so he could take a short break. I agreed, which meant that I was now responsible for pouring and mixing drinks for the customers. Ordinarily, that would be fine, but I struggled to tend bar while under the influence of this new experience. I felt paranoid, and it seemed like I was taking giant steps when I walked. I was pouring three times the amount of alcohol into each drink than was normal and I felt like the customers were all staring at my every move. The fifteen minute break I had given David felt like an hour. Fortunately, I had the wherewithal to call David back and tell him, truthfully, that I was out of it. With this, he returned to tend the bar and I walked out of the club and went back to my apartment. That was my first and last drug experience.

My daughter, Sylvia, often dropped by to see me. She and Linda had become quite friendly. One day, Sylvia showed up and asked if she could speak with me privately. We went out to an ice cream parlor for sundaes and some father-daughter conversation.

Sylvia and I had always had a good rapport and it continued in spite of my separation from her mother and my crazy lifestyle. We spoke for quite a while about what was going on in her life and then she switched the conversation to her mother.

My estranged wife, JoAnn, was scheduled to go into the hospital soon for surgery. I told Sylvia that I would visit with her mother the next day.

I felt that I should help out while JoAnn was ill, as she and Sylvia were in Phoenix and far away from the family support network of the North End.

I spoke with Linda about this but she was against me being part of JoAnn's support network. Needless to say, our relationship ended. It really seemed like the best decision for all concerned. Being with Linda had been fun, but the longer I knew her, the more I realized that we were really from two different worlds. I told Jim Sanders that I was moving home to help out, and that I would be out of the apartment by the end of the month. Linda moved out and went to live with her sister on the west side of Phoenix. Jim Sanders and his significant other, Shane, decided to get married and take over the whole apartment. Within a short period of time I was back home with JoAnn and Sylvia. It was time for me to put my crazy lifestyle behind me, and be with my wife and daughter. I had been adrift for awhile. People handle adversity in different ways. I am proud that I managed to get back onto the right path.

Eddie Connors

Even though I lived in Arizona for nineteen years, Boston was always home to me. It was important for me to know what was going on back home, so I got into the habit of regularly reading the Boston newspapers. I picked up the Boston Globe one day and was shocked to find a crime story focused on an old friend and sparring partner, Eddie Connors. A tough kid from Boston's Dorchester section, Eddie had apparently gotten mixed up with the wrong crowd. He had been gunned down gangland style in front of a phone booth in Boston.

Eddie and I had been friends since we were teenagers, and I was saddened to learn how violently his life had ended. I didn't focus on who killed Eddie or why he was killed, but thought only of the loss of my good friend. We had sparred many times in the ring and would always head out for coffee and conversation afterward. We shared stories about fights, conditioning, and our lives as young men growing up on the streets of Boston. Although I was from the Italian neighborhood and Eddie was from the Irish section of the city, our lives had many similarities. When Eddie and I boxed on the same card, we would meet before fight time and walk to a church to pray for good things to come our way.

I had been fighting as a headliner long before Eddie Connors entered the sport but in the fight profession, you never know who your next opponent will be. Persistence paid off for Eddie. He was scheduled to fight me in a lucrative bout at the Boston Garden on April 20, 1959. I was a better fighter than he was, even at the tail end of my career, but Eddie was tough. Growing up in the streets of Dorchester, you had to be tough.

That match went the full ten rounds without a knockdown, but I won by unanimous decision. There was never any animosity between us. We were pals. In fact, Eddie personally had a tape made of the fight and sent me a copy after I moved to Phoenix.

A few years later when we both had retired from the ring, Eddie bought a bar in the Savin Hill neighborhood of Dorchester, an Irish stronghold then and now. At that time, I was working in the liquor distribution business. Without hesitation, Eddie made sure that I supplied him with most of his liquor needs. Eddie Connors was a good friend. Unfortunately, like some other friends from my old neighborhood, Eddie could not escape the arms of the underworld, and eventually paid the price.

Fight Night, USA

Marvin Hagler and Vito Antuofermo were boxing for the middleweight championship of the world in Las Vegas. Al Siciliano and I decided to show up for the bout. Ringside, it seemed like Hollywood and Washington all rolled up into one. There were movie stars, singers, comedians, producers, directors and an array of politicians from the nation's capital.

The Speaker of the House of Representatives, Thomas "Tip" O'Neil was at the fight. He was one of the most influential people in America at that time. O'Neil always looked out for the people of Massachusetts. What was in their best interests was in his best interest. He had a saying that has always stayed with me, and most politicians agree with it, "All politics are local."

I knew Tip O'Neil from the old days. He had followed my career in the ring and I had watched him rise in politics, first in Massachusetts, then nationally, and finally as Speaker of the House of Representatives. Unlike many politicians, he was a sincere, regular guy. If Tip befriended you, he would go out of his way to help without looking for anything in return. This is a rarity in the political spectrum.

Tip and I spoke in the back of the hall before Hagler and Antuofermo appeared for the main event. He had heard of Vincent's death, and knew he was my only son. After Tip asked how things were going, he put his arm around my shoulder and I knew what he meant. I replied that I was doing okay, and then he asked about my daughter, Sylvia. He mentioned that he had an internship in his office in Washington for her if she was interested. When I later told Sylvia, she was thrilled and accepted the position.

The conversations then turned to Joseph DeNucci. Tip knew that Joe had been a stable mate of mine when he was in the ring. He mentioned that Joe was making a name for himself as a member of the Massachusetts House of Representatives, and that he was likely to advance to the chairmanship of the Committee on Human Services and Elderly Affairs. I agreed that Joe was indeed a remarkable person and he had the guts and brains to support his dreams. As the fights were about to begin, Speaker O'Neil motioned that he was going to head to his seat and told me that I'd be hearing from him.

The preliminary fights on the card were fairly good, but the main event, which was an exciting battle between Hagler and Antuofermo ended up in a draw. This meant that Antuofermo retained his World Middleweight Championship title. Hagler, however, would be back. He not only became one of the greatest middleweights of all time, he also became a dear friend.

At The Sands

I continued to spend a lot of time in Las Vegas. Vic Damone was headlining at the Copa Room of the Sands Hotel and I wanted to see him perform. When my friends and I arrived for the show, someone must have recognized me. Before I knew it, I heard two names being called to stand and take bows. The first was Johnny Puelo, the leader of a nightclub act called The Harmonicats. They were a harmonica group that injected comedy into their performances thanks to Johnny, who was a little person. They became popular after several appearances on the "Ed Sullivan Show." The second to be introduced was yours truly. After the show, I had the opportunity to speak with Johnny and discovered that he grew up

In Vegas with Wayne Newton.

in Boston's North End. I had never known him in the old neighborhood, as he was much older than I was. We talked about the old days, growing up Italian and some of the characters who came from the same streets we called home.

Early the next evening, Al Siciliano dropped by with Joe Curtis, a friend who worked in public relations. Joe had also been a referee at one point in his life and then went into the construction business, eventually owning his own company. We were invited to sit with Carl Cohen, the casino manager at the Sands. Cohen was a tough guy who was known to have a quick temper. He was actually the reason why Frank Sinatra, their number one headliner, canceled all of his future engagements at the Sands, and signed with Caesars Palace, the new multimillion dollar resort located diagonally across the Strip. Sinatra, who normally had a line of credit at the Sands Casino, was refused an extension of his credit line by Carl Cohen. Sinatra confronted Cohen about this refusal and an argument ensued followed by a fist fight that resulted in Cohen knocking out one of Sinatra's front teeth.

As we sat sipping our drinks, Joe Curtis spoke about an upcoming boxing exhibition he was planning that would feature some former champions and current rated fighters. He mentioned a star-studded show that would include Carmen Basilio and me as the welterweight opener and middleweights Jake LaMotta and Rocky Graziano as the main event. Other bouts included in his show would feature Billy Graham (the fighter, not the evangelist), Rocky Baronosky, Harry Krause, Gene Fullmer, Art Aragon, Joey Maxim, Joe DeJohn, and Joey Giambra. He also wanted to include a couple of transplants from the east coast, boys like Joe Volpe and Al Siciliano, both originally from Boston's North End.

Joe also mentioned that the card might feature former middleweight champion, Tony Zale and heavyweight contender, Lou Nova as the referees for the evening. There would be two masters of ceremonies, comedian Pat Cooper and singer Sonny King. As I listened to his grand plans, I hoped he knew what he was doing. Today, a card like this would cost about $100 million.

April 4, 1981 was set as the date for the boxing exhibition. The action would take place at the Frontier Hotel in Las Vegas and was billed as a salute to Joe Louis, the longest reigning heavyweight champion of the world. Louis was considered by some to have been the greatest fighter, ever.

Joe Louis had not fared well financially and owed the IRS several million dollars in back taxes. His financial dilemma was well documented. As a matter of fact, when Frank Sinatra signed to appear exclusively at Caesars Palace, one of his contract stipulations was that Joe Louis would be the greeter at the resort. He would stand outside the main entrance and say hello to the people walking through the front door. As part of the agreement, Louis was never to know that he was hired as part of Sinatra's contract to appear in the main supper club. Sinatra thought it would be embarrassing if Louis knew that his new position was the result of Sinatra's insistence and, while he was alive, the secret never leaked out.

When we arrived for the boxing exhibition we were greeted by the former champ. I thought he looked sickly. Louis perked up, and grinned from ear to ear, when we all shook hands. We didn't chat very long because of his weakened condition, but while we were there, all he did was smile. He was thrilled that the evening was a salute in his honor, and he was going to enjoy every minute of it. That night was special for everyone involved. We all felt proud to be part of it. The fights took place without a hitch, accompanied by the usual verbal jousting, creating an evening of sheer entertainment. After the exhibition, the entertainment changed focus as Joey Bishop, Pat Cooper, Sonny King, Bernie Allen and a host of others put on a show for us.

In addition to the boxing show, there was an auction of boxing memorabilia. One man was determined to outbid everyone for a Leroy Neiman portrait of Louis in action. Neiman, considered to be one of the premier sports artists, became famous for his artwork published in *Playboy Magazine*. The bidding went into thousands of dollars and that particular gentleman outbid everyone to acquire the painting. That man was the heavyweight champion of the world, Larry Holmes. After Joe Louis passed away, Holmes presented the portrait to the Louis family.

The End of a Chapter

Frank Capizzi and Frank Palermo, a couple of former North Enders from the old days, had relocated to Mesa, Arizona. I contacted them to reconnect, as we had very similar upbringings and backgrounds. One day a conversation I had with Frank turned to my goal of serving food at The Living Room. If I installed an oven in the kitchen, I would be able to serve food during the day and continue on with our lounge, featuring good, live music every night. After I did the math, I figured it could mean a possible increase in revenue of 25% if I could get an oven installed. If this plan worked, it could save the business.

Frank, a pipe fitter by trade, offered to do the necessary work in his spare time and when the job was completed, he wouldn't take a dime. I did well with the oven in operation during the daytime but, after a few months, business started to decline again. It seemed as though The Living Room had seen its day. I decided to re-evaluate my future. It was time to face the inevitable. I thought of selling out and heading back to Boston where I was sure I could find a decent job, but I wasn't sure what I should do. One Sunday afternoon, I called my old pal, Massachusetts State Representative Joe DeNucci. He was dismayed when I told him my business was not doing as well as it had before the reconstruction project. Access to the lounge was just too difficult.

Joe and I discussed the possibilities if I returned to Boston. It was the tail end of 1982 and I was almost 50 years old. I wasn't sure who might hire me, especially since I had been running my own business for so long. Joe assured me that because of my reputation as a fighter, as well as the fact that I managed to avoid any controversy or scandal over the years, I would have no problem securing a job. Joe mentioned that many people wanted me to succeed, because it would not only be good for me, but for the North End and the Italian community.

A few days later, Joe called me with a possible opportunity. He had contacted the Speaker of Massachusetts House of Representatives, Tommy McGee, who was very interested in helping me. Tom McGee asked Joe to give him a little time to work out a few things, and he would get in touch with me. Joe added that McGee was a big fight fan who thought that a position for me would be great for the Commonwealth.

About a week later, Joe DeNucci called and told me that if I came home, I would be appointed as a court officer for the General Court of the House of Representatives in Boston. "Just sell out in Phoenix, return to Boston and you'll be all set. Congratulations."

When the moving vans arrived, The Living Room still had two years left on the lease. I called a business friend, Scotty McGinnis, to ask his opinion about selling the business. Scotty was a crop duster during the day and a musician at night. He often sang, yodeled and played guitar for my Sunday night celebrity showcase. I sought out his opinion because he had a keen business sense. Scotty advised me to consult with an experienced business broker to evaluate what I had to offer. The sale would be for the furnishings, the inventory and the remaining two years of the lease. My biggest asset, he said, was my Arizona liquor license. I knew that Scotty had hit the nail on the head but I just wanted to hear it to help with my decision. I followed his suggestions to the letter and a month later, the lounge was sold. I was about to leave The Living Room behind after a fourteen-year run. Most of the memories I would always cherish. Some, I would try to erase.

The day I closed the lounge a group of my closest friends and I went out to Nick Marchese's bar on North 16th Street in Phoenix to celebrate. I was one of Nick's first customers when he opened and we had been close friends for eighteen years. The gang and I decided to have the final blast where it all began, at Marchese's place. My days in Phoenix were ending forever.

Round 12

Home Sweet Home

I had mixed emotions as I sat silently looking out of the window of the aircraft that brought us back to Boston. JoAnn and Sylvia had fallen asleep. I just stared out at the clouds, thinking all the while about leaving Phoenix. A good part of my life had been left behind there. I would miss the climate, The Living Room, and the friends that were with me in good times, and in bad. As I sat in the plane worrying about whether or not I made the right move, I thought about a saying my mother used when life's circumstances became stressful; "God closes one door and opens another one." I hoped that her wisdom would ring true on yet another venture in my life. Only time would tell.

As soon as we arrived in Boston the search began for a place to live. We had all gotten used to suburban living so we really didn't want to move back to the North End. After several weeks of searching for a house, we found the place we wanted. It was a sprawling, waterfront home located in North Weymouth, an upscale community a few miles south of Boston. Not only did we fall in love with the house, we found everything else to be captivating. Our new home was situated on a hill that rolled down to the waters of Wessagusset Beach. There was a panoramic view of Boston Harbor and the buildings of the downtown section of the city. We had a huge picture window that faced northeast revealing Boston's Logan Airport. From this direction, we could watch the planes take off and land, yet we were far enough away that the noises of air travel did not disturb us. What pleased me the most was that we were only twelve miles from where I would be working in downtown Boston.

Tommy Heinsohn with Sylvia and me.

Sylvia soon began working at the Boston Computer Exchange on Temple Street which was located in the shopping area of the city, just a block away from Boston Common, America's oldest public park. I worked on the other side of the Common, at the State House, an impressive gold domed Federalist building located on Beacon Hill. My job was to keep order during public sessions of the House of Representatives. This meant that when the house was in session and the public was allowed to be present, I was to make sure that proper decorum was displayed at all time. I was sworn in by the House Speaker McGee and soon learned how the state government was run; with bills being introduced, scrutinized and submitted to the members for their votes. In the process, I met many politicians, lobbyists and business people of all types. The experience was fascinating and I would spend the next fifteen years loving my job.

One day I received a distressing emergency phone call. Sylvia had severely injured her back falling down the stairs at the Boston Computer Exchange. Within minutes, I ran across Boston Common to Temple Street arriving at my daughter's side, not knowing what to expect. Sylvia asked me to take her to a hospital complaining about the pain in her back.

She was seen at the emergency unit within minutes of our arrival. After a thorough examination, the attending physician confirmed that Sylvia's back injuries were severe. She would be incapacitated for months and not be able to return to work.

To complicate things, JoAnn and I were drifting apart. We had tried reconciliation but it wasn't working out the way we had hoped it would. In retrospect, tragedy and hardship can either bring a couple close together or further apart. Unfortunately, instead of growing together, we were going in separate directions. JoAnn filed for a divorce and after thirty years of marriage, it was granted by a Boston judge. I was going to start yet another new chapter in my life. JoAnn was awarded the house in Weymouth as part of the settlement. Sylvia stayed with her while I moved closer to Boston. I found an apartment I liked in Somerville, a blue-collar community located right next to the city. In spite of the split and the distance between where we now lived, I continued to be very involved in Sylvia's care, as her injured back was not improving.

A Day with Dapper

Soon after my return to Boston, I received a phone call from the grand marshal of Boston's Columbus Day Parade. He asked me to participate in the parade on October 12th, stating that I could either walk or ride the parade route while waving to the spectators. This was quite an honor as the Boston Columbus Day Parade is one of the oldest Columbus Day celebrations in the United States. The first Boston event took place in 1910 on Tremont Street, but over the years a tradition evolved that the parade would rotate between the two big Italian neighborhoods of Boston. That tradition has continued to this day, with the parade in the North End one year and in East Boston the next. The year I began to participate, the parade was scheduled for East Boston.

When I arrived at the starting point to receive parade instructions, I was in good company. Many local and state politicians were marching that day, including Albert "Dapper" O'Neil. A well-known Boston City Councilor, Dapper was planning to march that day as he had not been assigned to ride in any vehicle. I decided to offer him a ride in the car that had been provided for me by George D'Amelio, an old friend and North End restaurateur. Dapper took one look at the pristine, white 1966 Cadillac Eldorado convertible and agreed to join me. There was plenty of room for both of us to sit comfortably, up high on the rear seat of the vehicle, while we waved to the crowds as we passed by.

The parade route began on Bennington Street in Orient Heights, an affluent section of East Boston, and continued west to Maverick Square, a commercial plaza that ends where Boston Harbor begins. The crowd was enormous and they all cheered as we rode down Bennington Street into Day Square and then onto Chelsea Street, a wide residential thoroughfare that leads right into Maverick Square. As we passed by, people shouted from the sidewalks, the windows of their apartments, and the rooftops of the buildings, "Dapper, Dapper, Dapper." The cheers continued from the beginning of the parade until it ended. I was humbled by this outpouring of support for my parade companion. It was obvious that Dapper was one of the most loved and most colorful city councilors Boston ever had. An old fashioned politician who called it like it was, Dapper championed the Bostonians who felt powerless, and because of this, his reputation preceded him everywhere he went. Although I have participated in the Columbus Day Parade many times since, riding the parade route with Dapper at my side will always stand out as the most memorable.

An Event at Foxwoods

A new phenomenon was taking place across the country. Indian tribes were legally able to operate gambling casinos on their reservation land. They took full advantage of this new ruling by opening several resorts that were modeled after the Las Vegas casinos. Foxwoods Resort Casino, located in Ledyard, Connecticut, was just a short drive from Boston, making it a popular gambling destination. Along with the casino, Foxwoods also offered entertainment and special events, including prize fighting.

I first learned of this when I received a phone call from Rip Valenti's grandson, Al Valenti, who invited me down to Connecticut. A well-known boxing promoter, Al was planning an extraordinary three-day promotional event at Foxwoods, and he wanted me to participate. It would consist of ten world boxing champions, all of them of Italian descent. This would be something unique as it would be a first for this type of event. I was the one Al contacted first as he and I had kept in good touch over the years. We got together at his Canal Street office in Boston to discuss the other champs he was considering for the event. Among them was Sal Bartolo, a Champion in the Featherweight Division. At that point in time, he was the proprietor of Sal Bartolo's Ringside Café in East Boston. Sal had won the title in 1946. Another participant was to be the great Willie Pep, who won the Featherweight Championship in 1942. He lived in Hartford, Connecticut which was conveniently close to Foxwoods.

Al also wanted to include Vinnie Pazienza, the "Pazmanian Devil," who lived in Rhode Island. He was easy to reach as he did a lot of public relations work for Foxwoods. The popular and famous Jake LaMotta had already been contacted and had agreed to participate. After his autobiography was made into the movie "Raging Bull," Jake's popularity had a huge resurgence. What increased the notoriety surrounding his great career in the ring was the fact that Robert DeNiro received the Academy Award for Best Actor in his portrayal of Jake.

Joey Giardello, the Middleweight Champion in 1963, was invited to participate. He won the title from Dick Tiger and had beaten Sugar Ray Robinson in a non-title fight. At one time, he actually held two undisputed titles and retired with 101 victories.

Al continued to tell me the names of the others who would be at the event. My old pal, Carmen Basilio, "The Onion Farmer" would be there

The two old warriors, friends forever. Tony and Carmen.

along with Light Heavyweight Champion Bobby Czyz, who had become a radio and television commentator. Rounding out the lineup would be Junior Middleweight Champion Vito Antuofermo and former Lightweight Champion Ray "Boom-Boom" Mancini.

Finally the first day of the event arrived and it was "old home week" for all the fighters involved. We shook hands, hugged and swapped war stories until we were hoarse. Foxwoods began the three-day event with a Memorabilia Evening, which was held in the main banquet hall. There were many photos of the ten champions along with hundreds of new boxing gloves and punching bags. They were all for sale, to be autographed by the fighters. People crowded in wanting to meet the former champions and to buy autographed memorabilia. At one point, there must have been a few hundred people waiting in line for autographs, and to pick up articles and biographies on their favorite fighters. All of the champions were sitting at a long table, lined up for the fans to speak with and to get their items signed.

Foxwoods is a casino and we all know the main business of a casino is gambling. I had never been opposed to a game of chance, having indulged many a time back in the days when I lived fairly close to Las Vegas. My game was always craps. I also like to play blackjack and even a slot machine or two. However, as part of the boxing weekend, Al Valenti told us we were to play a promotional game for charity. It was called "Texas Hold 'Em." I didn't know the technical rules and aspects of the game but to me, I figured poker is poker.

It seemed like fun; it was for a good cause, so I was in. Participating along with me were Sal Bartolo, Jake LaMotta, Vinny Pazienza and some of Foxwoods' high rollers. The game lasted an hour and a half, and without knowing the rules, I won all of the chips. In the very last hand, Vinnie raised me because he thought he had a winner. I countered with a raise and displayed a straight flush. For you non-gamblers, that is a hand of cards in numerical order and of the same suit. I won the last pot, which contained a total of $100,000. I wish I could have kept the winnings, but since I was playing for charity, I gave it all back. It was a real kick to win that amount of money though.

Later that evening, I was playing craps in the "no smoking" part of the casino. As I looked up from my position at the end of the table, I glanced at the large screen television about fifty feet away, only to see myself slugging it out with Carmen Basilio. Even though I had seen the fight so many times, it was enough to distract me at the table. I continued placing my bets with my eyes fixed on the fight. Why? I don't know. It's not as if I won that fight. This didn't do my chances much good as far as winning at craps was concerned either.

An acquaintance from Providence, Rhode Island was standing next to me. None of my close friends were watching the fight, so I started a running commentary on the fight with this guy from Providence. The other players at the table were stuck listening to me describe the fight. Those who were not fight fans must have thought that I wasn't all there. But, for me, as Yogi Berra once said, "It was déjà vu, all over again."

Dead or Alive?

Art Aragon, a west coast boxer nicknamed the "Golden Boy," called me and told me how great it was to hear my voice, and he wasn't kidding. The tone of his voice sounded rather strange. Art and I were friends but not real buddies like some of the guys I had grown up with so, I asked him what was wrong. He replied that a reporter from the *Los Angeles Times* had called him to verify a report that I had died in a Los Angeles hotel room. Art told the reporter that he had just seen me a few weeks earlier, but that he would call and check in with me. After we chatted for a few minutes, Art got in touch with the newspaper to let them know I was alive and well in Boston. Upon hearing that "THE" Tony DeMarco was alive and well, the reporter from the *Los Angeles Times*, contacted me for an interview. When he called, my only comment was, "No, I'm not dead. My health couldn't be better." Following that brief interview, I called Art Aragon and asked him to check the Los Angeles newspapers on the following day just to make sure I wasn't dead. He called me a couple of days later to read me this article from the *Los Angeles Times*:

"TONY DEMARCO NOT DEAD, NOT EVEN KO'D"
September 12, 1990 / Earl Gustkey / Times Staff Writer
"A report circulated Thursday that Tony DeMarco, a prominent boxer in the 1950s, was lying in a county morgue, his body unclaimed. A call went out to another prominent boxer of that period, Art Aragon. "Impossible," Aragon said. "I just saw Tony two weeks ago and he

was fine. But let me call him to check and I'll call you right back." According to Aragon, the following conversation took place with DeMarco, who lives in Boston:

DeMarco: *"Tony DeMarco speaking."*

Aragon: *"Tony, this is Art Aragon. The L.A. Times says you're dead--are you?"*

DeMarco: *"Geez, I don't know…let me go look in the mirror. (Pause). No, I'm still here, Art."*

Turns out the deceased, Alphonsus D'Amico, had passed himself off as Tony DeMarco for two years at a downtown bar, where he was a frequent patron. When he failed to appear at the bar for several days, the bartender reported Tony DeMarco missing to the police, who found D'Amico dead of natural causes in his downtown hotel room.

DeMarco, 58, world welterweight champion in 1955, was amused by the mistaken identity when contacted Tuesday. "My health couldn't be better…but I told Aragon I'd check the obituaries in the paper tomorrow, just to make sure. "

Staying Connected

When it comes to a sport that creates comrades, it is boxing. The individual clubs are called Rings after the Square Ring that we are all familiar with, and there are at least one hundred Rings in existence.

The Massachusetts Association of Ring started in 1947, and is considered one of the oldest in America. Mass Rings are quite active, in fact, there are three groups located in within the Commonwealth. One of the club's functions is to protect the dignity of the sport and the boxing community; past, present and future.

As a result of the Ring, I became friends with many of the old timers who were retired before my days in the ring. Included in the list is Mickey Finn, president of the Veteran Boxers Association, Ring 4, along with "Iron Mike" Pusateri, not to be confused with "Iron Mike" Tyson. In his day, Mike was managed by Rocky Marciano's corner man, Al Columbo. Mike belongs to all three Massachusetts Ring Associations and continues to keep me involved with the organization's activities.

***

The Champs. Joey Maxim, Willie Pep, me, Joey Giardello, Carmen Basilio.

After a wonderful run working at the State House, I finally decided to retire and enjoy my friends and family. I got into the habit of joining the guys from the old neighborhood for breakfast at the Meadow Glen Mall in Medford, a city just west of Boston. We would always have a great time reminiscing about the old days over coffee and donuts. My old pal Lou Vivolo was a staple at our daily haunt, but after a while stopped showing up.

It was October, and I was scheduled to march in the Christopher Columbus Parade again. This time I was asked to march with the Greater Boston Renaissance Lodge of the Sons of Italy, which was presided over by Dr. Dean Saluti. The members of the Renaissance Lodge are all professional people: lawyers, judges, college professors, CEOs of industry and people who network at these levels. I felt honored to be marching with them. As we paraded in East Boston on Bennington Street through Orient Heights, I heard a familiar voice call my name. When I looked over, I saw the Vivolo family in front of their house, waving and calling to me. I spotted Lou's wife and daughter and yelled, "Where's Lou?" Lou's wife yelled

Dottie and me on the parade route.

back, "He's been sick." I made a snap decision to leave the parade, calling over to Dean Saluti, "Dean, tell Christopher Columbus I'll be right back." When I got to Lou's house, his wife told me that he was housebound and had been ill for a long time.

I stopped in to say hello to Lou and his brother Armando, a former boxer whom I had known from my ring days in Boston. I wished Lou well and told him I would save his chair for him in the Mall until he was ready to return to our breakfast group. They asked me to join them for lunch but I had to return to the parade. I joined up with the closest group from the Sons of Italy Lodge and continued marching. I didn't catch up to Dean Saluti until we disbanded at the end of the parade route. I told him that I had wanted to continue marching with the Renaissance Lodge but they were too far ahead when I was able to rejoin the parade. I then explained the situation as it developed. He understood and all was well on Columbus Day that year.

***

Over the years I participated in many parades. Several years later I was named Grand Marshall of the North End Athletic Association Christmas Parade. This is an event that is timed to kick off the holiday season in the North End section of the city. Santa Claus is flown in by helicopter to start the festivities. Each year, a grand marshal is picked to lead off the parade and I was pleased that my old neighborhood chose me for that special honor in 2004. I received a phone call one morning from the association; "We would like the pleasure of having 'The Flame and Fury of Fleet Street' to lead the way this year." I replied, "The pleasure would be mine." I agreed to meet with their committee at the Nazzaro Center where my boxing life started.

Many pictures were taken, and added into a compilation of photos from the old days, including shots of houses and restaurants in the North End. As the event began, association president, Dom Campochiaro, took command. Along with Robert "Ted" Tomasone, one of the originators of the association, Dom directed Santa as he exited the helicopter at the North End Park located on the waterfront of the neighborhood. Dom and Ted then coordinated the sections of the parade as we kicked off the celebration by marching through one of Boston's oldest neighborhoods.

The Breakfast Club

The Meadow Glen Mall in Medford became a morning ritual. Guys from the North End, West End and East Boston would gather in the food court every day. We would push a few tables together and spend a couple of hours sipping coffee and reminiscing about the "old days." One morning, we discovered that one of our breakfast club members had passed away. Tony Campo was a former fighter who was beloved by our morning crowd. When it came time for his farewell, there was a special Mass in his honor at the Sacred Heart Parish in Medford.

Many of Tony's old friends from his childhood on Clark Street in the North End were in attendance, as were people from all over the North End. All of his old pals from the breakfast club showed up, and were greeted by Father Meskell, the pastor of the church. Before the funeral ceremony began, he walked around the church and stopped at the rear where we were sitting. The pastor was looking for some information that he could add to Tony's eulogy. The guys spoke about where Campo grew up, his boxing career and what he did after he retired from the ring.

Father Meskell was amazed to learn there were eight professional boxers from Clark Street in the North End. He wrote down all their names starting with Tony Campo and then added in Frankie Ross, Joe Beans, Freddie Farr, Ronnie Mason, Tony Nogueira, Al Sforza and Jackie Lupo. During his sermon, Father Meskell acknowledged Tony Campo's family sitting in the first pew and then the rest of us sitting in the rear of the church.

When it was time in the service for Holy Communion, the pastor made a point to walk to the rear of the church and tell the guys that he had the authority to forgive their sins if they chose to take the Holy Eucharist. Some of them hadn't been to church in many years, so this became quite an event. The guys thought getting their sins forgiven was a pretty good deal, so most of them took the pastor up on his offer. Shorty McDuff was the only one who was uncertain about receiving communion. He thought he might take it home to his wife and actually tried to put the Host in his pocket. Father Meskell stopped him saying that what he was trying to do was sacrilegious. He backed off and swallowed the Host, as did the rest of us.

When the service was over, the guys met in front of the church. We were all in our 60s, 70s and 80s. Shorty was very emotional, stating that he hadn't received Communion for over thirty-five years; it felt good to have his sins forgiven and get back in the fold. Tony Nogueira revealed that for him, it had been twenty years and that the priest had made him feel comfortable enough to try it. The Ciccarelli brothers and the oldest member of the group, Joe "Yo Yo" Arria, all said they thought it was Tony Campo, himself, who made this happen. Afterward, we all embraced with a true feeling of camaraderie. Believe me, the confessions would have been priceless if the priest got to hear them.

***

After many years of family life, it sure was lonely living alone. I discovered that hanging around with the guys only goes so far. After JoAnn and I divorced, I started to date again but no one really interested me. Don't get me wrong, I met some very nice women. I would take them to dinner, a sporting event or to a club where the entertainment was quiet enough to allow for conversation. The whole dating game seemed superficial to me. I was just going through the motions but was secretly hoping for more.

This all changed one evening at a social function when a mutual friend introduced me to Ann Marie Martara. We clicked right away, and because of Ann Marie, I began to enjoy life again. She lived in an apartment located in the prestigious high-rise Prudential Tower condominium complex in Boston's Back Bay, one of the best neighborhoods in the city. When I saw her apartment, it became obvious to me that Ann Marie was very artistic and had excellent taste. The interior décor, furniture, colors, accessories and everything she chose blended together perfectly. I was impressed by her talent for creating an attractive yet comfortable environment.

At the time, I was renting a plush loft in Medford conveniently close to the Meadow Glen Mall where I met the boys for breakfast. As Ann Marie helped me decorate my place, I was fascinated to see the rooms of my loft come to life. She introduced me to the arts scene in Boston, while I introduced her to boxing and the other major sports that the city is famous for. Even though we were from two different worlds, we were compatible and always enjoyed our time together.

I was happy to take Ann Marie to functions hosted by the organization I belonged to as she seemed to fit in wherever we socialized. She was equally comfortable mingling with people in the society columns and people in the sports section of the newspaper. She was the right girl at the right time for me.

The Organizations that I Love

George Randazzo, founder of the National Italian American Sports Hall of Fame, called me one day in 1987 to solicit my support in starting a new chapter of the NIASHF to be located in Boston. Ten years earlier, while living in Phoenix, I had attended the Chicago function that launched the national organization for the sport of boxing only. In 1978, the mission of the organization broadened to recognize athletes of Italian descent from all major sports. NIASHF honored Joe DiMaggio, the legendary "Yankee Clipper" that year among other standout athletes. I was thrilled to be inducted into the National Italian American Sports Hall of Fame in 1981.

As an NIASHF honoree now living in Boston, George looked to me to help start the new local chapter. I was always happy to lend my support to charitable organizations such as the Muscular Dystrophy Foundation, American Heart Association, Veteran Boxing Association, Renaissance Lodge of the Sons of Italy as well as the Pirandello Lyceum, an organization honoring Italian Americans who have excelled in their field of endeavor. George Randazzo's request struck a cord with me and I decided to help him out.

My first call was to an old friend, Freddie Corangleo. As a youth, he was quite an athlete. He later worked with children as a teacher and counselor, but after developing muscular dystrophy he was confined to a wheel chair. This certainly didn't slow him down. Freddie had a positive attitude, a quick mind, and lots of connections. He was just the guy to get the New England chapter of NIASHF off the ground. Freddie agreed to get involved and became the first treasurer of the New England chapter.

Freddie successfully recruited distinguished, capable members to the board of directors including Sal Balsamo, founder and CEO of TAC Worldwide, and Dave Gemelli, President and CEO of Gem Gravure Company, along with several other prominent businessmen.

I then decided to reach out to Rip Valenti's grandson, Al Valenti. He was a boxing promoter just like his grandfather, but had expanded his horizons to include show business. Between Freddie, Al and his father, we soon had a mailing list that spread the word and membership started to build immediately.

My pal Joe DeNucci also decided to get involved. After retiring from the ring, Joe entered politics. At that point in his career, Joe was a state legislator and Chairman of the House of Representatives Committee on Human Services and Elderly Affairs. He became the first Chairman of the Board of the New England Chapter of the NIASHF.

A personal phone call from me to former Governor and Secretary of Transportation, John A. Volpe resulted in his acceptance of the position of Honorary Chairman of the Board. The New England Chapter of the National Italian American Sports Hall of Fame quickly became quite influential, not only within the Italian community but with everyone involved in sports in Massachusetts. The endowment for scholarships alone soon exceeded three million dollars.

A few years later, in 1990, I was honored by being inducted into our local New England Chapter of the NIASHF. I was in great company as the New England Chapter also recognized several other local greats that year. Red Sox great Tony Conigliaro, former Undefeated Heavyweight Champion of the World Rocky Marciano, and boxer Johnny Wilson (Giovanni Panica) were all honored with posthumous inductions. Other living legends inducted that year include Gino Cappelletti, Joe Bellino, Donna Caponi, Dom DiMaggio, and Phil Esposito.

***

One of my greatest moments came several years later, when I was honored in my own neighborhood by the City of Boston. A group of people led by a dear friend and former boxer, Nick Sullo, along with Jim Tubarosa, petitioned the City to co-name Fleet Street, the street that I grew up on, Tony DeMarco Way. Mayor Thomas Menino hosted a gala ceremony with the unveiling of the new street sign. I am proud even to this day that the very street that I grew up on is now named after me.

If you have ever been to the North End, you would know that parking is at a premium to say the least. When I was asked to speak, I thanked everyone in the city for the great honor. I then turned to the Mayor and asked, in jest, if a parking space came with the street sign. Without missing a beat, in Italian, the Mayor responded *scordatilla* which basically means forgetaboutit!

***

Through my work with several charitable organizations in the Boston area, I met attorney and entrepreneur Francis D. Privitera. He invited me to the annual May breakfast function sponsored by the Sons of Italy Commission for Social Justice. The event was held that year at the Marriott Hotel in Burlington, Massachusetts, a northwestern suburb of Boston. The organization is the local chapter of the National Commission for Social Justice of the OSIA, Order Sons of Italy America. With the mission to insure equal treatment, respect and opportunity for all people, it opposes all stereotyping of ethnic, racial, cultural and religious groups especially as depicted by the mass media in America.

There were four attorneys at the Privitera table, Frank, his daughter Jeannine, and his sons Frank Jr. and Philip. Frank's wife, Jean, proudly participated surrounded by her extraordinary family. I suppose if I needed legal advice, I would never have to travel very far. I certainly didn't need any advice when I met Roseann Spinale that day. She was donating her time to sell raffle tickets at the Sons of Italy breakfast. I found her to be very attractive and was immediately interested. At that point, my relationship with Ann Marie had become stale. Although neither one of us wanted to admit it, we both know the relationship had run its course. When Roseann approached me for an autograph to be raffled off later in the day, we hit it off immediately, and chatted for quite a while. There was definitely a mutual attraction and we exchanged phone numbers before the breakfast came to an end.

Roseann was a talented artist who had the polish and sophistication that I admired in a woman. She owned a two hundred year old home in Marblehead, an affluent seaside community a few miles north of Boston. Her home was filled with antiques and her own artwork which she sold in a store located on her property. For the next few years we were inseparable. We attended functions sponsored by all of the organizations we were involved in. Roseann was especially helpful when I accepted the various tasks offered me by the many charities I had committed myself to. Although we were close, Roseann understood that my heart was with the welfare and health of Sylvia. Life was very busy, but I was happy.

My New Home

My daughter Sylvia and I had noticed a new condominium building being constructed on Staniford Street in Boston's old West End. Actually, this location was central to Government Center and directly across from the Thomas P. O'Neill Federal building. The Boston Garden (at that time called the Fleet Center) was right around the corner. The old Garden was one of America's first indoor sports and entertainment arenas. Not only was it home to the Boston Celtics and Boston Bruins, but as I have already mentioned, it was the venue for most of my professional championship fights. I was very interested in moving back to the city, and got in touch with Frank Viola to learn more about the condo project. Frank was well known in the business since he had taken over Haymarket Cooperative Bank from his dad. The close proximity to the Garden, Government Center, and my old North End neighborhood was very appealing to me.

As part of Boston's "Big Dig" transit project, the overhead train rails and highway superstructure that divided the West End neighborhood were demolished. The revitalization plan identified areas for development and the neighborhood began to go upscale. As the condo complex approached completion, I called the number listed on a sign that advertised rentals and purchases.

Today I am living in that condo at West End Place as a result of that call. The condo has many features that are very appealing and the proximity to the entire city is perfect. It is just a few blocks away from the State House, Fanueil Hall, Government Center, the Charles River and the North End. I can walk to any of these places in a few minutes. Boston is a walking city, and since I was a kid, I have always preferred to walk to my destination. It's large enough to be cosmopolitan but small enough to be intimate. When tourists follow the Freedom Trail to see the landmarks of colonial Boston, they can do it all on foot.

My daughter Sylvia had been temporarily living with her boyfriend's aunt in Dedham, a community just south of Boston. My plan was for Sylvia to move into the new condo with me. She was elated when she heard that we would be moving into the new building, located right in the middle of the city. I described the place to her in detail, and how the construction of the building was progressing. She was thrilled and just smiled.

Everything began falling into place and we moved in as soon as the construction was completed. Because we were so close to the North End, Lou Lanci, Peter Cantelone and many more of my friends would drop by to see the new condo and visit with Sylvia and me. Peter was a self-taught but talented artist. Sylvia was delighted when he gave her a sketch she admired of Mother Teresa and she immediately hung it on her bedroom wall.

Dottie

Even though I had many responsibilities between my job, charities, and social organizations, I still considered Sylvia to be my first obligation. She was 36 years old in 1999, but she had never fully recovered from the fall she had taken at work in 1992. I brought her from doctor to doctor for consultations but her condition had only worsened over the years. Sylvia was restricted from driving and many other activities that might tire or weaken her. Her boyfriend, Chuck, was very dedicated. He gave Sylvia a ride home from work every day and would run errands for her. He cared for her every minute, and I truly admired him for this type of commitment.

One April day in 1999, my sister Josephine called to see if we could get together that evening, as we hadn't seen each other for several months. We planned to meet at Moseley's on the Charles, an old fashioned ballroom located in Dedham right on the Charles River. This would be a convenient halfway point between Medway, where Josephine lived, and Boston. As I already had other commitments, Josephine and I decided to get together early in the evening for just a few hours.

I arrived a little early and enjoyed listening to the band while I waited for Josephine. The name on the music stand read, "Johnny Shea and his Orchestra." Their music was reminiscent of the big band era and couples were gliding across the dance floor to the melodies of songs like Moonlight Serenade, Chattanooga Choo Choo and Begin the Beguine.

My concentration on the music was broken when my sister Jo arrived with two of her friends, June and Dottie. They were lovely ladies who joined in as my sister and I caught up on family news and events of the day. One of Jo's friends intrigued me to the point that I did something rather unprecedented. I asked her to dance. The band played a couple of romantic ballads and, as I looked at my partner Dottie, a feeling of contentment and security came over me. Although I had been dating Roseann Spinale, and later dated Janet O'Brien, I couldn't get Dottie out of my mind.

Not long after that chance meeting, I introduced Dottie to my daughter. Sylvia and Dottie hit if off immediately, which made me very happy. I soon got up the nerve to tell Dottie how I felt about her and discovered that she felt the same way about me. That was the beginning of a long, loving relationship with Dottie. I had finally found the woman who would complete me.

My Darling Daughter

I was becoming very concerned about Sylvia because she was showing no signs of improvement, and actually seemed to be getting worse. Dr. Richard Winickoff's office was close to our new condo and Sylvia chose him as her primary care physician. A well-respected physician, Dr. Winickoff suspected that Sylvia had issues that went beyond her back problems. There were other things that did not seem right and needed to be investigated. He recommended that she be seen by specialists at Massachusetts General Hospital. She was seen by Dr. Leonard Appleman, another noted physician who ordered a battery of tests to try to identify the underlying problem. After the test results came back and were evaluated, Dr. Appleman determined that my daughter had developed myelodysplasia, a form of leukemia. With that diagnosis, once again my world was shattered.

Sylvia needed a bone marrow transplant. Unfortunately, neither her mother nor I was a match. A few months passed and Sylvia's health continued to deteriorate as we waited for a compatible donor. Without a bone marrow transplant, the myelodysplasia would quickly become acute leukemia, which would shorten Sylvia's life expectancy to no more than a year.

Time was running out. A second opinion with another specialist or

My darling daughter, Sylvia.

specialists was imperative. Physicians familiar with Sylvia's medical condition set up a meeting at the Dana-Farber Cancer Institute located in the Fenway section of Boston. This included cancer specialist Dr. Joseph Antin and Dr. Appleman from Massachusetts General Hospital. JoAnn and I were in attendance along with Arthur Schurliff, a social worker who had been consulting with Sylvia. Dr. Antin's recommendation was to hold back on the bone marrow transplant until the infections Sylvia had developed had been treated and were reduced to safe levels.

Since JoAnn was living in Hernando Beach, Florida, she thought it would be beneficial to Sylvia's health if she spent some time with her mother in a warmer climate. After she was settled in with her mother, Sylvia saw yet another doctor who recommended a more aggressive treatment in the form of chemotherapy. Unfortunately, the treatments drained Sylvia's strength. I kept in constant touch by phone every day, but one day, Sylvia called; "I need you, Dad." Sylvia had never asked anything of me in the past and I immediately knew that I had to get right down there. This was destined to be our last phone call.

Dottie was in the travel business so she was able to get me on a flight to Florida immediately. My sister Josephine insisted on going with me, and I was very glad to have her along for moral support. Just before we left, I received a call from JoAnn to tell me that Sylvia had been rushed to the hospital. We went directly from the airport to the hospital where we learned that Sylvia's condition was grave. The attending doctors admitted that there was nothing more they could do for her and it was decided that Sylvia would be released from the hospital.

The comfort of her immediate family was Sylvia's final blessing. My beautiful daughter died later that night surrounded by all of us. I couldn't help but think that no parent should outlive their children. This was the second time in my life I had lost a child and there is no way to describe the pain, anguish and helplessness I felt. It was unbearable.

The memorial service and funeral were held in Inverness, Florida. It meant a lot to us that a number of Sylvia's friends, aunts, and uncles made the trip to Florida to pay their respects. I decided to have a memorial Mass in Boston for those who couldn't make the trip to Florida. Having time to grieve with loved ones is so important. Following the services, I hosted a dinner for the mourners at Filippo Ristorante, one of Boston's nicest establishments. Filippo Frattaroli, the owner, personally supervised the preparations and table service to make sure I was satisfied with everything. I was grateful that so many of my friends and relatives attended. Their presence at the service was something I will never forget.

The Journey Continues

For the next several years, life was very difficult to bear. If it were not for Dottie, Josephine and my lifelong friends, I don't know what I would have done.

As I began to come out of my period of mourning, Dottie and I started to get out more. One night we decided to go to a nightclub to see two old friends who were appearing at the Matrix, a local Boston nightspot. Angelo Boncore and Vinnie Calderone were original members of the Hi-Lo Trio, a vocal jazz group that was quite popular in the 1950s and 1960s. I had seen them perform years before at the famed Latin Quarter, a huge Boston nightclub originally owned by Lou Walters, the father of Barbara Walters.

The Hi-Lo Trio had long since broken up and at that point Angelo and Vinnie were working as a duo. They played the Ritz Brothers as the opening act for the hilarious Joey and Maria's Comedy Wedding. My two old friends were very comical as was the entire cast from the bridal party to the in-laws and the priest who was called Pastor Fasioli. Actually, the entire cast was named after types of Italian pasta including "Don Ziti," the Godfather.

Audience participation was part of the overall script, and the Godfather was usually chosen from their numbers. That evening, the privilege was reserved for me. With my public speaking experience, which included sports nights and a few TV interviews, I proved to be an adequate Godfather. Angelo and Vinnie quickly scripted my lines.

The show continued and everyone played his or her part quite naturally. I felt I did well as everyone told me my timing was just perfect. After the show, the management offered me the opportunity to act on a regular basis in the role of the bride's father, "Tony Cavatelli." I now had a new pasta alias that I could add to a long list of aliases from my boxing years I was now Tony DeMarco, "actor."

***

One warm spring evening, not long after my baptism as a stage performer, I was in downtown Boston and decided to take the subway home. I rode the "T" from the Boylston Street Station to North Station, and exited in front of the Boston Garden. From there it was a short walk to my condo at West End Place and to Dottie.

For the entire time it took me to walk those few blocks, I thought about all of the names and nicknames I had used or were attached to me during my life. I started out Leonardo Liotta, and then became Chubby, Lenny and Leo before I was known as Tony DeMarco and was called TD, The Flame and The Fury, Champ and a few other names, some worth forgetting. All of them combined, reminded me of who I was and where I came from.

I have experienced some great things in my life. In the boxing ring I was able to accomplish what few men were able to do back then. I can say that I was the undisputed champion. I never forgot my roots, my friends, or my family. I made some very good decisions in my life but I also made some mistakes. We all do. I was able to reach the top of the mountain, while always staying true to my roots. I will always be the kid from Fleet Street. I am thankful to God for giving me such a rich life. I have been blessed.

I thought about all of the events that shaped my life. The boxing game is not quite the same today, but in the end you have two warriors striving for victory. Sometimes in order to get that final victory, you must face astounding odds. In my heart, I believe I was able to do exactly that, and in the end I was victorious.

As I continued with my walk to my condo, I heard a shout from across the street. The Venezia girls, Lillian and Anna, sisters whom I had known since I was a kid, spotted me and yelled out with an echo, "Naaardo." I looked up, smiled and waved back.

The Players

Tony DeMarco fought eight world champions, and had fifty-eight wins, thirty-two of them by knockout. In addition to fighting twice at Fenway Park, beating both George Araujo and Vince Martinez, Tony holds the record for the most fights and most sellouts at the Boston Garden. His epic fight with Basilio in 1955 was named fight of the year by *The Ring Magazine*.

Rocky Marciano retired as the only undefeated heavyweight champion of all time, with forty-nine wins, forty-three of them by knockout. The Brockton Blockbuster was tragically killed in a plane crash on August 31, 1969.

Carmen Basilio became a world champion in both the welterweight and middleweight divisions. He fought eight world champs and won fifty-six fights. Carmen has always remained a true friend and gentleman.

Johnny Saxton won fifty-five of his sixty-six fights over a great career, beating Kid Gavilan for the welterweight championship. He encountered some difficult times after he retired, and passed away in October of 2008 in a nursing home in Florida.

Vince Martinez had an illustrious twelve-year career, but was never able to win a world championship. He fought the best and was considered one of the best. Vince passed away on January 29, 2003.

George Araujo was another tough customer who lost his championship quest to Jimmy Carter. A skilled boxer, he passed away in 1997.

Rip Valenti went on to become a very successful promoter, working with the likes of Ali, and Frazier. He also managed the great career of Joe DeNucci. His grandson, Al, has carried on the family tradition.

Sammy Fuller went on to train Joe DeNucci as a middleweight along with a number of other boxers. Sammy passed away in 1979.

Phil Buccola retired to Sicily after the government targeted him as the head of the Mafia in New England. Phil continued to correspond with his successor in the states who he hand picked. His successor was Raymond Patriarca. Phil lived to the ripe old age of 101. Raymond died in 1984 while under indictment for mob activities in New England.

Joe DeNucci went on to fight some of the greatest of all time. He lost his bid for the middleweight championship against the great Emile Griffith on two occasions. Joe went on to a distinguished career serving in the Massachusetts House of Representatives. He was House Chairman of the Joint Committee on Human Services before he became the longest tenured State Auditor in Massachusetts history.

Cal Bellavia, Bobby "Ames" Agrippino, Frankie "Ross" Toscano, "Smeaky" Pasquale, Dante and Benny DeChristoforo, the Sica family, Sal "Fernando" Cardone, Barney Lanci, Jerry Tecce, Berrio Gizzi, Sonny King, Lindy DeChristoforo, Guy Consolo, Frankie Campbell, Jim Spero, Al Siciliano, Lou Lanci...the list goes on and on; too many to name. They were all a big part of my life. Suffice it to say that they helped me to the top of the mountain and when I stumbled, they were there to pick me up. For that I am forever grateful.

Epilogue

Tony still lives in the West End of Boston in the same condominium with his lovely wife Dottie, and their two cats. He has become the unofficial ambassador for Boston's Italian North End, chatting with tourists and residents alike

The Sports Museum in Boston recently unveiled a new Tony DeMarco exhibit located in the TD Bank Garden, which sits on the site of the old Boston Garden where Tony won his championship. There is also talk of a statue of Tony that will be erected in the North End.

As a tribute to Tony, a beautiful mural of him was commissioned, along with a plaque commemorating his years in Phoenix. The mural was

My love, Dottie.

created on a building at the corner of Camelback and 40th Street, the site of the old Living Room. He is also a member of the World Boxing Hall of Fame.

Still very connected to the community, Tony is involved with many organizations such as the Italian American Sports Hall of Fame, the Sons of Italy, Ring Four and the Veteran Boxing Association. You can still find him once in awhile holding court at Foxwoods Resort and Casino.

Tony DeMarco Way is the major cross thoroughfare in the North End. Tourists love to take a picture of the street sign, and some are even lucky enough to get a picture with the Champ when he is there chatting with friends and visitors.

Also involved in the Boston entertainment circuit, Tony still appears in Joey and Maria's Wedding and various other productions. He is still sought after as a speaker at many events, and even has his own Facebook Page: TKO Tony DeMarco.

Lastly, Tony still hangs with the gang most days. Together they solve the world problems, have a few laughs, enjoy a donut and coffee, all while keeping the tradition and memories of the old days alive.

Me and the rest of the cast from Joey and Maria's Comedy Italian Wedding.

I will always remember.

Marquis Book Printing Inc.

Québec, Canada
2011